Walking Away a
WINNER

With Fasting, Praying, and Giving

Deborah Morgan Bush

Contents

Dedication

In memory of my father, Peter H. Morgan Jr.

You left fingerprints of grace and giving in my

life. You will never be forgotten.

Especially for you!

Introduction

Prayer and fasting led to the writing of this book. I genuinely desired a deeper intimacy and response from the Lord. To know His perfect will in my life I often dedicate twenty-one days at a time for fasting and prayer. This is my secret to obtaining open doors, miraculous provision, favor and that sweet fragrance of God upon my life and my family. Let fasting become a lifestyle. As I sat down to write the impact that fasting, praying and giving has had in my life and personal ministry over the years, I am at a loss to summarize it. How can I explain what it means to have intimacy with God and input from

Him on a daily basis? How can I explain in words His ways of giving me visions and dreams and then clarifying it over and over to me? How can I explain a continual flow of answered prayer? All I can do is give you a few strokes on my laptop and highlight the impressions He places on my heart. The Lord impressed on my heart, saying, "When you write, you move the promises of God into the future." I pray that He will somehow use this book in your life as a challenge to take you to Him at His Word, obey Him by faith and move forward step by step in obedience. This book was inspired during a fast and written for you and your family, perhaps a friend or neighbor. Now, I invite you to join this miraculous journey. I pray that each person reading this book will be covered with the blood of Jesus, that eyes will be opened. Scales will fall off eyes and hearts. Restoration, renewal, new revelations, ideas, goals, plans for the future, healing of mind, body and soul, and deliverances from strong-holds will come forth. That you will become so blessed that you will enjoy giving it away. In Jesus' name, AMEN

In reading this book, you will notice that I believe the Word of God is a truth that justifies all that I have put into this. Everything written is supported by His Word to bring you a future and hope. Let's start with a few scriptures to set the tone in place.

John 1:1, In the beginning was the Word, and the Word was with God, and the Word was God.

Romans 15:4, For whatsoever things were written aforetime were written for our learning, that we through patience and comfort of the scriptures might have hope.

John 8:32, And ye shall know the truth, and the truth shall make you free.

Revelation 1:3, Blessed is he that readeth, and they that hear the words of this prophecy, and keep those things which are written therein, for the time is at hand.

Psalms 147:5, Great is our Lord, and of great power; His understanding is infinite.

Revelation 12:11, And they overcame him by the blood of the lamb, and by the word of their testimony; and they loved not their lives unto the death.

Jeremiah 17:7, Blessed is the man that trusteth in the Lord, and whose hope the Lord is.

Acts 6:4, But we will give ourselves continually to prayer, and to the ministry of the word.

Chapter 1

Fasting to Win

Having proved the great value and blessings of fasting over many years, I really wanted to share this experience with those who hunger for God's best in their lives and the lives of those they love. Fasting is important, it's more important than many of us have ever known. Jesus said, "Blessed are those who hunger and thirst for righteousness, for they shall be filled." (Matthew 5:6) Hungry people are desperate people. They are hungry for more of God than they realize. Fasting stirs a hunger in the spirit that goes deeper than the temporary hunger you experience in your flesh. When you hunger for God, He will break the rules of man and cause His favor to come on your life. To show God you are serious, you must get to the point where you are desperate for God. You must desire Him more than food, drink, social media, or addictions. When you hunger for God, He will fill you. So let's get filled with the bread of His presence!

Fasting with a pure heart and the right motive provides us with a key to unlock doors where other keys have failed. A window will open up new horizons in the unseen world. A spiritual weapon of God's providing. Fasting, praying, and giving, whether corporately or individually, is a personal sacrifice. Where there is little private discipline, there is little public reward. It is a sacrifice born out of expectancy, but not a manipulative tool to get something out of God. "But a reasonable act of service," (Romans 12:1) that God rewards openly.

Fasting is a personal matter between man and God. Fasting, like prayer, must be God-initiated and God-ordained if it is to be effective. God places a burden on us through the Holy Spirit and we respond to that burden. Prayer that originates with God always returns to God. Set your fasting and prayer apart for God. This is an absolute basic if our fasting is to be accept-able to Him. Simply stated, biblical fasting is refraining from food or pleasure for a spiritual purpose. "And we know that God causes every-thing to work together for the good of those who love God and are called according to His pur-pose for them." (Romans 8:28)

In biblical times it was normal to fast because people needed an answer. They needed to win a war, to save a nation, or for healing and release from demonic strongholds. When you fast and pray you are giving heaven notice that you are truly in earnest and that you will not let go, nor let God go without the blessing. You do not intend to take no for an answer. God chose to make fasting His way to make His voice be heard on high. When you begin to honor God with fasting, praying, and giving, you will see for yourself that it is directly linked to prosperity, financial freedom and healing.

"If you do these things, your salvation will come like the dawn, yes; your healing will come quickly. Your godliness will lead you forward, and the glory of the Lord will protect you from behind. Then when you call the Lord will answer. Yes, I am here, he will quickly reply." (Isaiah 58:8, 9) Fasting humbles you and brings clarity. Forgiveness and bitterness flee from your heart. It will also overcome sexual addictions and demonic powers such as pornography, adultery, fornication and lust, thus breaking great sin off people.

It is a privilege to fast, pray and give. It is a powerful weapon to our spiritual armor. Increasingly large portions of the population are hopelessly bound by nicotine, alcohol, drugs, sex, and gambling. Others are deceived and entangled by satanically inspired societies, cults, witchcraft, and black magic. Some Christians are bound by fear, resentment, jealousy, uncleanliness, depression and despair. They try very hard to pray and believe, but yet they are bound unable to fast, pray, and give effectively.

When you stop something or deprive yourself for the purpose of fasting, your mind becomes uncluttered from the things of this world and amazingly sensitive to the things of God. You will enter into a deeper, more intimate and powerful relationship with the Lord. There are dimensions that the Lord will never reveal to the disinterested, casual worshiper. When you take steps to break out of the ordinary and worship Him with fasting, praying, and giving, you will break out of the ordinary and worship Him the way He deserves. He will begin to share secrets with you about Himself, His nature, His character, and His plans and desires for you and your family. Your enemies or circumstances may seem to be so large and powerful that they are all you can see, but when you worship, you not only magnify God, you also reduce the size and power of everything else around you. When you worship with fasting, praying, and giving, you magnify God.

Threefold Cord is not Quickly Broken

"A threefold cord is not quickly broken"

Ecclesiastes 4:12

When King Solomon was writing the books of wisdom for Israel, he made the point that a cord, or rope, braided with three stands, is not easily broken. There are three ways that you can practice this; by fasting, praying, and giving. When practiced together, they create a type of threefold strong cord that is not easily broken.

Are you wondering what blessings are not being released, what answers to prayer are not getting through, what bondages are not being broken? Have you exhausted every attempt with your life or the lives of your family members? If Jesus could have accomplished all that He came to do without fasting, then why did He fast? The Son of God fasted because He knew that there were supernatural things that could be released only that way. Whether you desire to be closer to God or you are in great need of breakthrough in your life, remember that nothing will be impossible to you. Fasting is a secret source of power!

Once you have made the decision to fast, even if it's for one day, God sees the desire of your heart. He will provide you with the grace to endure and see the breakthroughs you need to come to pass. You need to understand that God has some "promised lands" and some "promises" for you. Likewise, God wants to pour out supernatural blessings in our lives, but they will never be realized or released if we are not willing to seek Him in fasting, praying, and giving.

Now, get ready, there is never a "good time" to fast. God knows there is never a good time to fast or a "convenient" time to fast. There is always something standing in our way, whether it is our busy lives, a holiday, a birthday, an event, or money. There will always be something that creates a bump in the road, an obstacle that will try to talk us out of it.

The duration of your fast can vary. The Bible does state significant numbers. They include one day, three days, seven days, twenty-one days, and forty days. There is no real formula to determine the type or length of fast that is right for you. It depends on the circumstances. Don't get bogged down in the details. The details are not as important as your heart's desire to satisfy God with your sacrifice. Don't bite off more than you can handle. Don't be daring and attempt a forty-day fast if you have never fasted in your life. A fast needs to mean something. If it doesn't mean anything to you, then why do it? Without being combined with prayer and the

Word, it's just a diet or refraining from some-thing. Remember Matthew 6:33, "Seek first the kingdom of God and His righteousness and all these things shall be added unto you." If you seek Him first, get ready for all the joy and pros-perity that will be added to your life. You will dis-cover and realize that fasting itself is a continual prayer before God.

If we are not careful, we can allow life to get us into the same old routines and busyness without even realizing it. Our relationship with the Lord can suffer the same fate. What does it take to stay sharp and sensitive to the Holy Spirit? Our praise, worship, and giving can become heart-less routines to God. The busyness of life can bring you to the point of routine with mean-ingless sensitivity to the Holy Spirit and what pleases Him. There may be days when heaven opens and your heart is prompted to deep times of prayer and there might be other days when your energy is depleted and you cannot focus on prayer at all. Don't condemn yourself. God sees your sacrifice.

Men and women of God have fasted since ancient times. The Greek physician, Hippocrates, known as the "father of medicine," influenced the development of medical practices for centuries. He believed fasting was very healthy for the body. Today we have many books on the shelf about the health and physical benefits of fasting. Fasting can break the addictions to social media, Internet use, cell phone use, unhealthy eating habits, nicotine, alcohol, drugs, and other emotional factors. When you present your mind and body in this intimate manner, you open yourself up to hear from God. You will discover His good and perfect will for your life. Fasting is a tremendous weapon, a source of power. When you honor and worship God by presenting your body as a living sacrifice, then you will know His assignments for your life.

Perhaps you are at a place of such desperation that you just cannot afford to miss God's will for your life. I have known people who were literally facing life or death situations. They were trapped under the pressure by circumstances, under attack by the enemy (Satan). The only way they survived was by drawing near to God, listening to hear His voice, and following His plan. Remember, the enemy's agenda is to steal, kill, and destroy you (John 10:10). Do you think the enemy wants you to believe that nothing is impossible for you? The enemy knows he is defeated, but he doesn't want you to know it or to walk in that realm of God's power. That is why the enemy wants to distract you. Do not allow the enemies in your life to cause you to focus more on yourself or whatever you separated yourself from such as food, TV, internet, or friends more than on the promises of God that are released when you employ the powerful weapon of fasting. God takes notice. He sees the sacrifice you have made for Him. Get ready for the presence of Jesus like you never had before.

Fasting is not just a physical discipline; it can be a spiritual feast. Once you "taste and see that the Lord is good," (Psalms 34:8) His presence will eclipse the limitations of your understanding. God knows more about what you need than you do. Some of you may be battling with the same sins or you are trapped in bondages and strongholds that you have tried to eradicate, only to have them come back again and again. You may be living free from the effects of sin but see the cycle repeated in your children. It is a personal matter between you and God, in light of your needs and circumstances. It is important that you approach this spiritual fasting exercise with certain principles in mind in selecting the fast of God's choice for yourself and your family. Fasting can be individual or as a family. There are no age limits, but before you fast, ask yourself: Am I confident that this fast is God-given? What should I fast from? Food, coffee, soft drinks, TV, Internet, social media, or other pleasures that take up your time. Pray about which fast you should enter in with. Think about your motives. Is there a hidden desire that is not pleasing to God? Is your desire for personal blessings balanced by genuine concern for others? Can you worship and praise the Lord during this season of fasting? You should expect that a season of fasting would prove to be a time of conflict with the powers of darkness. Satan will often try to take advantage of your physical and spiritual condition to launch an attack on you. To avoid becoming discouraged and giving up, guard yourself with a spirit of praise and worship no matter what the enemy sets against you and your family. Before you fast, talk to your spiritual leader about fasting. Have a group of friends pray for you during your fast. Having accountability will help you during times of weakness or when the enemy tries to create doubt. Allow others to walk with you during a fast. Scripture tells us to surround ourselves with like-minded individuals. These people will be able to stand against the enemy when you start to feel that you cannot.

Remember, your Father who sees in secret rewards you. Read Ephesians chapter six in preparation to begin your journey. As you begin this life altering journey in prayer, the Holy Spirit will lead you in the specific instructions that will be unique to you regarding the type of fast and the length of the fast. This book is designed to guide you into fasting, praying and giving. You can adjust it to your fasting timeline that God places on your heart.

A fast is often determined by your circumstances and commitments. Sometimes the Lord directs you during the course of the fast to end it or extend it. Keep a journal of your day-to-day experiences, revelations, and ideas. Write down goals so you can refer back to it throughout the fast. When Satan begins to attack, write out your prayers against him. He knows breakthrough is on the horizon for you and he will try his best to distract you.

The purpose of a fast is not so much to receive but to give. Have your fast be an opportunity to give to the Lord. It is a time to intercede for your situation or circumstance, cooperating with God in the outworking of His plan. "We will have nothing to fear, provided we remain humble before God and are clad in the heavenly armor." (Ephesians 6) God did not design fasting to make us vulnerable to Satan. When you fast unto the Lord, making the ultimate sacrifice, this is disturbing to Satan. He knows the power, favor, and blessings that come from renewing yourself. Take one day at a time to avoid becoming discouraged. Take each emotion as it relates to you or someone you know before the Lord in prayer. Before you plunge into your journey, begin with prayer that leads up to your fast, then read His Word each day and reflect on the emotion and how it relates to your situation and circumstance. When you feel you are growing spiritually dry, experiencing a lack of provision, a feeling of distance from God or needing a direct answer from the Lord, that is when the discipline of fasting releases the anointing, the favor, and the blessings of God in your life. The Bible says, "Blessed are they that hunger and thirst for they shall be filled." (Matthew 5:6) Maybe you are reading this book because you are not content with the way your life is going. Maybe you know there is more, you know there is an assignment on your life and you know there are things that God desires to release in your life. Feel the desperation in your heart for those things and respond to the Holy Spirit.

Examining your motives and actions prior to and during your fast will keep you from sinning against the Lord. First, ask yourself if you have repented of all known sin. Then confess your sin as it occurs. God will reveal sin to you through His Spirit and His Word. Begin to implement those changes in the way He leads you. Fasting is a means to answered prayer, God will answer prayers according to His grace, but more than that, you will become more like Jesus. You will be renewed, and in turn, be constrained by the love of Christ to help reach what He has placed on your heart for Him. Remember, the Lord delights in blessing those who diligently seek Him. (Psalms 37:4)

The Lord will teach you how to listen more carefully and specifically to what He has for you and how to apply it in your daily life. You will become more spiritually alert and sensitive to God than ever before. Fasting, meditating and praying will give you a greater awareness, an alert mind, keen senses, and a spiritual receptivity to what God is doing in your life. He will set up divine appointments, place certain people in your path, give you ideas and creativity, open doors and shut doors. Try to maintain a posture of humility and servant hood to see a genuine move of God. Remember, Jesus reached for a towel to wash men's feet. He did this because the Lord works in all spectrums of people. Those who are already doing well in their lives and those who are not. In this process, God binds our hearts together and gives us a love for each other.

Fasting, praying and giving will revolutionize your life, your family, your work, and even your ministry. God will give you a life message that can be shared with one person, one situation, or throughout the world. There are no limits. All of this will happen as a result of obedience to God in your life. Obedience to fasting, prayer, and giving will provide the means for you and your family to do what God has called you to do.

As you fast, pray, and give, God will show you the areas in your life that are kept off limits to God and the ways you seek to control your life rather than let Him lead you. Any coldness in your heart melts during a fast and you become empowered and transformed to walk in His ways. We begin to realize that God puts His blessings on people of unity, asking that all who believe in Him would be one. God will meet you in a gracious and abundant way.

PUSH – Pray Until Something Happens. This reminds us of a woman in labor. She is instructed to push. Push until something happens. Pray until something happens. Push until the birth of a new resolution comes, answer to prayers, release from bondage, and the reasons that lead you to read this book and start your fast. When you become discouraged in your fast, continue to push through. You may want to write the words PUSH on sticky notes as encouragement and place in different locations in your home, work, or car to keep you on track. Perhaps you do not fast because you fear you will harm your body or cause undue stress. As He leads you to fast you will accomplish what thousands of others just like you have completed and what they thought was impossible. All of us are biblically called to fast. Jesus said, "When you fast," not "If you fast." (Matthew 6:16) Let the Holy Spirit guide you with the details. When things have not gone the way we feel they should have, the Lord will put upon us a fervent desire to do things His way and not man's way. "I know the plans I have for you, says the Lord, plans to prosper you and not harm you, plans to give you a hope and a future. Then you will call upon me, and I will listen to you. You will seek me and find me when you seek me with all your heart. I will be found by you declares the Lord." (Jeremiah 29: 11-14)

As the deer pants for water brooks, so my soul pants for you, O God. My soul thirsts for God, for the living God. When shall I come and appear before God? My tears have been my food day and night, while they continually say to me, "Where is thy God?" (Psalms 42:1-3.) This will become a way of life for you and your family. You will begin to understand the importance of sacrificing for the Lord.

As you read and begin your journey, you will begin to become aware of and address different emotions, strongholds, sin, and anguish, which can be removed from you or your circumstances during your fast. They are emotions that everyone experiences at some point in their lives or the lives of family members. Throughout the Bible there are stories of how men and women went through this and how the Lord got them out of their situation or circumstance and blessed them.

Key Points

Fasting stirs a hunger in the spirit that goes deeper than the temporary hunger you experience in your fresh. When you hunger for God, He will break the rules of man and cause His Favor to come on your life.

Write down some sins that you feel you need to confess.

Ask the Lord to forgive you of these specific sins and to reveal any other sins that you may commit without knowing.

Write down some reasons you want to fast.

Once you have made the decision to fast, even if it's for one day, God sees the desire of your heart. He will provide you with the grace to endure and see breakthroughs you need to come to pass.

Ask the Lord to reveal the type of fast and the length of the fast.

Who are you willing to talk to about your fast?

Use the next page to write down any thoughts you have on fasting so you can discuss them with a spiritual leader or friend. Remember, accountability is the key to achieving goals.

Don't condemn yourself, God sees your sacrifice.

Fasting is not just a physical discipline; it can be a spiritual feast. Once you "taste and see that the Lord is good," His presence will eclipse the limitations of your understanding. God knows more about what you need than you do.

Fasting is a personal matter between the individual and God. Fasting, like prayer, must be God-initiated and God-ordained if it is to be effective. Remember, your father who sees in secret rewards you openly.

Are you ready to give Heaven notice? List your obstacles that are preventing you from offering your sacrifice of fasting unto the Lord.

Notes

Chapter 2

Prayer

How can I start to pray? I haven't prayed in a long time. My prayers are not effective. I feel lost in my prayer life. Are you feeling this way? Let's start from scratch with the Lord's Prayer. It does not matter if you have been praying all your life or you are just starting your prayer life.

Prayer is essential as a partnership with God, as a redeemed child of God, working hand in hand with God toward the realization of His redemptive purposes on earth. God works through the prayers of His people. From the time of creation, God chose to work on the earth through humans, not independent of them. He always has and always will, even at the cost of Him becoming human. Though God is sovereign and all-powerful, scripture clearly tells us that He limited Himself, concerning the affairs of earth, to working through humans.

Let's pray to the Father as Jesus taught in Matthew 6:9:

Our Father in heaven, may Your name be honored, May Your kingdom come soon. May Your will be done here on earth, as it is in heaven. Give us this day our daily bread. And forgive us our sins, just as we forgive those who have sinned against us. Lead us not into temptation, but deliver us from evil. For thine is the kingdom, and the power, and the glory forever, AMEN

Does He need us to ask for His kingdom to come, His will to be done? Surely He wouldn't want us to waste our time asking for something that was going to happen anyway, would He?

Didn't He tell us to ask for our daily bread? (Matthew 6:11) and yet, He knows our needs before we even ask.

Didn't He tell us to ask that laborers be sent into the harvest? (Matthew 9:38)

Didn't Paul say, "Pray for us that the Word of the Lord may spread rapidly and be glorified" (2 Thessalonians 3:1-5). Wasn't God already planning to do this?

Are not these things God's will? Then why am I supposed to ask Him for something He already wants to do, if it's not that my asking somehow releases Him to do it? It is sufficient to say that I believe our prayers do more than just petition the Father. I've become convinced that in some situations, prayer actually releases cumulative amounts of God's power until enough has been released to accomplish His will. Let's rise to this occasion and embrace the incredible invitation to be co-laborers with God and be carriers of His awesome Holy Spirit, and ambassadors for His great kingdom. Let's represent Him!

Awaken Us to Our Destiny, Lord!

The following is a weekly guide to praying daily during your fast along with the Lord's Prayer.

Sunday: Pray for favor with God. Seek His presence, His holiness, His anointing.

Monday: Pray for favor with others, including neighbors, coworkers, and lost people.

Tuesday: Pray for family, children, spouse, extended family and in-laws.

Wednesday: Pray for spirit, soul and body, your health, spiritual and physical wholeness.

Thursday: Pray for protection. Freedom from temptation, fear, deception, and your enemies.

Friday: Pray for finances, your priorities, your blessings, and becoming debt-free.

Saturday: Pray for increased vision, wisdom, guidance, dreams, plans, and ideas.

Continue this daily prayer guide each week that you fast. The Lord will impress upon your heart each day something new to pray about. Personalize it to your present and future needs and circumstances. It's going to be a surprise to you as the Lord plants a specific prayer request on your heart that you have never thought about on your own. Prayer is the proof that you respect God. It is a sign that you recognize His power to change your circumstance.

Praying will take you away from your immediate circumstance and expand you into a new prayer life. The burden that the Lord places on your heart will become a theme upon your heart. Years ago during a time of fasting, the Lord impressed upon my heart to pray for anyone who had been kidnapped or held against their will. I was surprised to know that I was to become a prayer warrior on behalf of kidnapped men, women, and children. How did this happen? I have never been exposed to kidnapped victims or have ever thought about this. But God saw that I could be trusted with this request and stand in the gap for these lost ones. Over the years I have seen many kidnapped victims found, discovered, and set free. I have also seen their captors discovered, uncovered, and exposed. If I wasn't seeking the Lord, I might have missed this awesome opportunity to be a part of this prayer request that was planted in my heart.

Ask God to open the eyes of your heart to hear from Him. The Lord may impress on you to pray for a particular nation, city, person, or even a ministry. He may also plant a desire that is very specific to a particular situation. It may be a need that may appear to be very small or something on a larger scale. Don't be intimated by the Lord's request placed on you, don't let satan take it and overwhelm you. Just do it and look for results!

Fasting and praying allows us to dwell with the Lord in the posture most pleasing to Him by intensifying in our hearts and bodies the qualities of humility, brokenness, and contrition. It will create in you a burning desire to draw near to God, to be cleansed of any impurity, and to be fashioned into a tool that God can use. Do you desire, by whatever means necessary, to be the salt and light to a dark culture, (Matthew 5:13-16) to obey God as He calls you to fast, pray and give? As you continue to read these pages, let your heart be filled with faith and hope. We serve an awesome God who longs to involve us in His plans; He is already up to something. Get ready!

If you have ever doubted that God works among His people today, prepare to have your mind changed and your faith dramatically expanded. God's power is indeed being poured out upon His people as a result of fasting, praying, and giving to seek God's face.

Humble yourself as you fast, pray, and seek God's face and turn from evil ways. He will begin to do great and mighty, even supernatural things with you. You and your family will begin to sense a sharpening of your spiritual faculties to become more in tune with what God is doing in you, in your family and throughout the world. God is waiting to bless and use you in unprecedented ways as you respond to His promptings to make fasting, praying, and giving a vital part of your life. As you apply your time in fasting and prayer, you will begin to feel results in a greater intimacy with God and a deeper enthusiasm for Him, which in turns spills over into every other area of life. The joy of the Lord will become more visible to others. People around you will take notice of something different, a change in your countenance as you're being prepared for what the Lord has for you. Fasting and praying prepares you for the harvest you are about to receive. You begin to turn away from the things that grab your attention and you begin to focus on the Lord. You will begin to realize how many tempting things of this world occupy your thoughts, time, activities, finances and even your talents. Are you willing to boldly turn from human interests and pleasures for a time? The point is, are we willing to lay them down at the feet of the Lord?

I am sure that no one needs to convince you that America and other nations are in need of prayer. We are seeing some of the worst corruption and immorality our nation has ever known. Wars, natural disasters, unemployment, and political unrest are on the news all day long. America is in danger of losing its very soul. Ordinary, casual prayers will not overcome the evil in our land. As you fast and give of yourself, you will also see clear signs that God is ready to bless and minister to all those affected by these issues in our land. It prepares their hearts to receive what the Lord has for them. Don't let what is happening in this world distract you from your quest to hear from God. As these things occur, ask the Lord to send His laborers into these areas to minister to those in need.

Sometimes the media has a way of creating fear and discouragement. These events are presented to us in many ways and many times over and over by the media. Pray over what the Lord impresses on you. Trust that His will is done in those areas and refocus on what the Lord has given to you to cover in prayer. Remember during your fast, life will go on. Carry on your usual family activities, work, and maintain your usual routine. "The Lord is good to those whose hope is in him, to the one who seeks him; it is good to wait quietly for the salvation of the Lord." (Lamentations 3:25, 26)

As humans and imperfect parents, we sacrifice to care for our children and meet their needs. Even in our imperfection, when our children ask for something special that we know would be good for them, we may wait for the right time to give it to them. We watch to see if they obey us and do the work we have asked them to do. We check on the way they treat their brothers and sisters. Sometimes we want them to ask us over a period of time so we are sure that their desires have not changed. We may foresee a good opportunity that the child cannot understand. I can only assume this is how our Heavenly Father regards our desire for more of Him. He is looking, checking, and listening. His timing is perfect. We cannot earn it, but we can demonstrate to our Father that we are ready; willing to do whatever it takes, fervently desiring Him. Let us beware of a spiritual arrogance that blocks out anyone who doesn't look or act the way we do. "The Lord does not look at the things man looks at. Man looks at the outward

appearance, but the Lord looks at the heart."
(1 Samuel 16:7)

Love in Jesus' name does not force others
into our own agenda. Are you willing to give up
your comfort zone? Drop your religious jargon?
Open yourselves to other ways of doing things?
The Lord will put upon you a fervent desire to do
things His way and not man's way. Satan is not
happy with this. You may begin to experience
spiritual warfare and it may intensify dramatically
in certain circumstances as satan seems to try
to find a foothold in your life or your family members. The enemy is trying to rob you of your victory. It's really important for people to complete
their designated time of fasting and realize that
you have stirred up a hornets' nest. The Lord
will reorder everything. With a spirit of humility,
you may suddenly find yourself changing almost
every one of your prayers, often with deep tears

as everything is focused away from us and for the sake of His name towards the need presented to us. You will soon discover that fasting and praying will become a foundation of almost everything you are doing.

We begin by humbling ourselves through fasting and prayer. If we fast and pray, it changes our sensitivity, our behavior, our thoughts, our relationships, our business plans, and our leisure pursuits. If there is no change in our lives, quite honestly, fasting can be a waste of time. In fasting, our Lord meets us and lifts our heads and sets us on a higher path. (Psalms 3:3) It is an amazing and wonderful experience that I pray each and every one of you can have.

However, as we see from Jesus' fast, the end of the fast is the time when the evil one strikes. Satan will try to trip you up at your weakest point just so you doubt the brokenness and spiritual work accomplished through your extended fast. You may then see yourself as worse off than before the fast. You may see yourself as unworthy to be used of God. You have to prepare for this attack. Just when you may be tempted to put up your spiritual feet to rest, you should put on your armor instead. Jesus warned his disciples, "Get up and pray so that you will not fall into temptation." (Luke 22:46) Temptation or persecution may come during your fast, three months later or even a year later. Even Jesus was tempted during His fast, but He quoted scripture. Satan wants you to feel as though you have failed in your walk with the Lord or that whatever you experienced during the fast was not real. Pray ahead of time and be prepared if you stumble. Remember that we are not condemned. Christ intercedes for us in all things. Confess, get up, brush yourself off and pick up where you left off.

Do not be tempted to do a slow slide to mediocrity or hardness.

The key is being in love with Christ Jesus and really believing that we can love people into His kingdom through the enabling of the Holy Spirit. Fasting humbles us and enhances our intimacy and trust in our Lord and King. It returns us to our first love so that we can love God and others deeply. No matter what happens as a result of fasting and prayer with the moving of the Holy Spirit, let Christ be the judge of all things. We, on the other hand, must remain faithful to loving, obeying, serving, giving, praising, and doing whatever He has called us to do for Him. Pray that God will consume your heart so that He can use you fully. The greatest love story of your life will be between you and Jesus.

We are only His instruments, trying to remain faithful to His calling. If we should ever make the prideful mistake of thinking we can do it ourselves, He could quickly remove His hand of blessing from us. God uses the humble, broken, obedient, and surrendered heart. He does not use a proud, boastful heart. We know more than ever, we must be on our knees before Him in a spirit of confession, humility, and obedience to His will.

Pray also that you will not be tempted to think of yourself as "super spiritual" because you completed a fast. Let us never forget that if the Lord had not brought us through it, we would not have made it nor experienced Him in our fasting. It would have been a mere work of our flesh. My prayer is that no one will even think that they are further along spiritually because they fasted more than someone else, or gave up something bigger or more significant than someone else. The point is to humble ourselves and stay humble!

The Word of God

Let's read a few scriptures concerning His Word

"The law of the Lord is perfect, converting the soul, the testimony of the Lord is sure, making wise the simple. The statues of the Lord are right, rejoicing the heart: The commandment of the Lord is pure, enlightening the eyes." (Psalms 19:7, 8)

"He sent His Word, and healed them, and delivered them from their destructions." (Psalms 107:20)

"Blessed are the undefiled in the way, who walk in the law of the Lord. Blessed are they that keep His testimonies and that seek Him with the whole heart. Wherewithal shall a young man cleanse his way? By taking heed thereto according to thy word. And I will walk at liberty; for I seek thy precepts. This is comfort in my affliction: for thy word hath quickened." (Psalms 119: 2, 9, 45, 50)

"So shall my word be that goeth forth out of my mouth; it shall not return unto me void, but it shall accomplish that which I please, and it shall prosper in the thing whereto I sent it." (Isaiah 55:11)

"Thy words were found, and I did eat them; and thy word was unto me the joy and rejoicing of mine heart; for I am called by thy name, O Lord God.'(Jeremiah 15:16)

Favor of the Lord

Let's read a few scriptures concerning Favor

"And I will make of thee a great nation, and I will bless thee, and make thy name great, and thou shalt be a blessing." (Genesis 12:2)

"For thou, Lord, wilt bless the righteous; with favour wilt thou compass him as with a shield." (Psalms 5:12)

"For His anger endureth but a moment; in His favor is life; weeping may endure for a night, but joy cometh in the morning. Lord, by thy favor thou hast made my mountain to stand strong; thou didst hide thy face, and I was troubled." (Psalms 30:5, 7)

"So shalt thou find favor and good understanding in the sight of God and man." (Proverbs 3:4)

"For whoso findeth me findeth life, and shall obtain favor of the Lord." (Proverbs 8:35)

"In the light of the king's countenance is life; and his favor is as a cloud of the latter rain." (Proverbs 16:15)

Fear

Let's read a few scriptures concerning freedom from fear

"God is our refuge and strength, a very present help in trouble. Therefore will not we fear, though the earth be removed, and though the mountains be carried into the midst of the sea." (Psalms 46:1, 2)

"What time I am afraid, I will trust in thee. In God I will praise His word, in God I have put my trust; I will not fear what flesh can do unto me. When I cry unto thee, then shall mine enemies turn back; this I know; for God is for me." (Psalms 56:3, 4, 9)

"The Lord is on my side; I will not fear; what can man do to me?" (Psalms 118:6)

"But the Lord is faithful, who shall establish you, and keep you from evil." (2 Thessalonians 3:3)

"For God has not given us a spirit of fear; but of power, and of love, and of a sound mind." (2 Timothy 1:7)

Prayer is the Answer

"The effectual fervent prayer of a righteous person availeth much." (James 5:16)

Pray first, plan second.

God expects us to be orderly. He expects us to manage our time, to discipline ourselves, to prepare well planned events in our life and the lives of our families. If we learn to pray first and plan second, how different would our homes, workplace, clubs, schools and churches be?

Sometimes we are planning in one direction and God's will is in another direction. God might say, "Hold everything! Turn around and go this way, this is my will for you, not that way."

Even if we are plugged into God's will and know we're going in the right direction, we may be going at a snail's pace. God wants us to make ourselves available to Him, and to say before we start to plan, "Lord, tell me what you want me to do, where you want me to go, and how do you want me to do it." Then our awesome God, with all the abundance of heaven at its disposal, will pour out His power on us. Instead of following our tiny plans, God wants to open heaven and flood us.

It's so Simple, Just a Conversation with God

When people start praying to "Our Father which art in heaven" in the name of Jesus, things begin to change. Our lives change, our workplace changes, our families change. Changes take place, not when we study about prayer, not when we talk about it, not even when we memorize beautiful scriptures about it. It is when we actually pray that things begin to happen. We don't suffer the "analysis of paralysis." We are not paralyzed by analyzing prayer, but we take the problems at hand and pray about them. This is what makes it exciting. We learn not about prayer, but to pray, to converse with our Father who is in heaven.

Praying in God's will is not easy, but yet it's very simple. It involves a commitment of every single thing that comes into our lives for God and His perfect will. It is exciting to live in a complete oneness with the will of God. It is never dull or static because it is not a one time, once for all commitment. It is something we have to work at constantly, moment by moment. Praying in the "Will of God" means being conformed to the will of God as we pray. Wouldn't it be great if we could always be conformed to the "Will of God," with all known sin confessed, so that we would never pray outside the "will of God"?

The Lord's Prayer really comes into focus right where we are when we pray. "Thy will be done on earth as it is in heaven"? Is there anything contrary to God's will in heaven? No! Have you come to the place in your life where you can say, "Lord, not my will, but Thy will be done. No matter how much it hurts, how difficult the task, how high the mountain you've given me to climb, it doesn't make any difference, dear Lord, I am willing"? O God, I want only Your will in my life. Open the doors You have for me, and give me courage and faith to go through them. In Jesus' name, AMEN

The Old Testament was based upon obedience to the written law of God, recorded in the five books of Moses called the Torah. The New Testament is based upon walking in repentance and forgiveness and acting upon the promises given. "If you abide in me, and my words abide in you, ye shall ask what ye will, and it shall be done unto you." (John 15:7)

Live every day with the expectation that you will fulfill your God-given assignment and live out all of your days. Seize the promise of Psalm 91:16: "With long life I will satisfy Him and shew Him my salvation."

There are times when you hear a message from God's Word and you are intellectually motivated. At other times, you are uplifted, encouraged, and blessed. There are occasions when the Word of God pierces into your soul like a sword and discerns your thoughts and the intentions of your heart. There are times you are hearing or reading a book that seems to come alive in your spirit. The truth seems to jump from the pages and suddenly you can sense inwardly a strong witness that God will move on your behalf. When the written or spoken Word of God becomes alive and energized in your heart, it is called "a rhema word" The word "rhema" is one of the Greek words translated in the New Testament as "Word of God." Also meaning a "thing said," or "utterance."

"So then faith cometh by hearing, and hearing by the Word (rhema) of God." (Romans 10:17) "And take the helmet of salvation, and the sword of the Spirit, which is the Word (rhema) of God." (Ephesians 6:17)

When the Word of God moves in your spirit, then faith will enter your spirit. You are able to believe what God has spoken and respond to His Word in faith. "Be careful for nothing, (anxious) but in everything, by prayer and supplication with thanksgiving, let your requests be made known unto God." (Philippians 4:6)

It is a privilege to see God being glorified in our lives. We are to give thanks always, knowing that we have a God who never makes a mistake. We need to be thankful in our hearts if we are going to be effective at praying in the will of God, and not just something we tack on to the end of our prayers. It is a commitment to God's will, a way of life. It is being in agreement for His will in the things for which we are praying and in our personal lives. "Giving thanks always for all things unto God and the Father in the name of our Lord Jesus Christ." (Ephesians 5:20)

Think of the most important thing in the world to you. It may be health, a loved one, job, finances, education, etc. Now pray, "Father, I want Your will in this thing or person that is most important in the world to me." Now in prayer, thank God for however He chooses to answer, knowing it is according to His perfect will.

Key Points

Prayer is essential as a partnership with God, as a redeemed child of God, working hand in hand with God toward the realization of His redemptive purposes on earth.

God works through the prayers of His people.

List some specific things or people you would like to pray for.

What is one way you have seen God work in your life through prayer?

Who are some people that you can ask to pray for you when you are in need?

Love in Jesus' name does not force others into our agenda.

The key is being in love with Christ Jesus and really believing that we can love people into His kingdom through enabling of the Holy Spirit.

Pray first, plan second.

It's so simple, just a conversation with God.

Praying is a commitment of every single thing that comes into our lives.

Have you come to the place in your life where you can say, "Lord, not my will, but Thy will be done?"

Rise to this occasion and embrace the incredible invitation to be co-laborers with God and be carriers of His awesome Holy Spirit. Prayer is the proof that you respect God.

List any hindrances to your pray life. What intimidates you?

Notes

Chapter 3

Forgiveness

$\mathcal{S}$ trife and confusion are a breeding ground that creates negative feelings toward others. Those feelings can lead to a root of bitterness that, when matured, produces the fruit of unforgiveness. Abiding in unforgiveness can give satan and his operatives an open door to take the unforgiving servant captive. The picture is clear; our own forgiveness is contingent upon our willingness to forgive those who have offended us. Christ took our sins for us and would not die on the cross until He prayed,

"Father, forgive them, for they know not what they do." (Luke 23:34) Christ Himself would not die with unforgiveness in His heart toward His enemies.

When Stephen was being stoned by religious zealots who believed they were doing God a favor in removing the scourge of Christian leaders from Jerusalem, Stephen cried out, "Lay not this sin to their charge." (Acts 7:60) If Jesus could forgive those crucifying Him and Stephen could pray for those murdering him, how much more can we forgive and release people who offended and wronged us?

If we willfully refuse to forgive, God cannot forgive us. Christ's warning implies that if we pray prayers with unforgiveness, our prayers are hindered. I believe the same is true with our spiritual warfare. How can a believer resist the enemy (James 4:7) and attempt to bind the powers of satan (Matthew 18:18) when the heart is holding grudges toward others in the body of Christ? If God does not hear our prayer, then satan is not obligated to hear our rebukes!

"If I regard iniquity in my heart, the Lord will not hear me." (Psalms 66:18)

God does not release us to pray for other needs until we clean up our lives by confessing our sins. You need to continue to pray, as God will keep bringing up sins to our minds. We all commit sins. What do we do with them? Do we live with them? The answer is that we get rid of them. God gives us the formula: "If we confess our sins, He is faithful and just to forgive us our sins, and to cleanse us from all unrighteousness." (1 John 1:9) All of us have blind spots, areas of sin we are not aware of. Those areas of sin hinder the work of the Spirit in our lives. Ask

God to reveal hidden sin. When God reveals sin, He also gives us grace to gain victory over it.

Dear Father, bring to my mind that particular sin or sins keeping You from hearing my prayers. I confess whatever You have brought to my mind as sin. Thank You, Lord, for cleansing me as You promised in 1 John 1:9 and qualifying me for effectual prayer. In Jesus' name, AMEN

"And forgive us our sins, just as we have forgiven those who have sinned against us." (Matthew 6:12) Your Bible translation may say debts or trespasses; both have the same literal meaning. Now, this is the Lord teaching us how to pray. Christ explained it like this: "Your Heavenly Father will forgive you if you forgive those who sin against you, but if you refuse to forgive them, He will not forgive you." (Matthew 6:14-15) The prerequisite to answered prayer is to forgive others, if we do not, our Heavenly

Father will not forgive us. If He does not, our sins will keep Him from hearing our prayers, and they will be of no avail.

Jesus also admonished His disciples, in rather strong words, "Listen to me! You can pray for anything, and if you believe, you have it, it's yours! But when you are praying, first forgive anyone you are holding a grudge against, so that your heavenly Father will forgive you your sins." (Mark 11:24-25)

One of the greatest hindrances to healing and answers to prayers is when unforgiveness blocks your spirit. When you do not forgive, you are holding people behind imaginary bars in your mental prison. Jesus Christ released you from a spiritual prison and an eternal destination of darkness and death. But we tend to take the offenders captive, refusing to talk to people who we don't like and even making negative comments about them in the presence of others. This is very displeasing to the Lord and a road-block on your journey. When you live with unfor-giveness toward others, you open a door for the very thing you are criticizing to come back on you. Bitter and angry words are compared to a tongue like a sword and arrows. When a person in secret shoots unfounded and critical words against another person, God says that He will make them stumble on their own tongue and they shall be wounded. (Psalm 64:2-8)

Forgiveness is required before you can enjoy emotional, spiritual and physical healing; forgive-ness is also linked to a person's freedom from any temptation. This is a direct connection to the Lord's Prayer. (Matthew 6:9-13) Each day, we should examine our motives, our hearts, and our relationship with God and with man. If we sin, the Holy Spirit will convict us with a strong burden and a feeling that we did something wrong. Once we confess, repent, and receive forgiveness, the conviction eases. Satan, however will often attempt to bring a feeling of condemnation and try to accuse us. This spiritual emotion can destroy our confidence in God's willingness to bless us. Without this confidence, our faith is weakened. "There is therefore now no condemnation to those who are in Christ Jesus, who do not walk according to the flesh, but according to the spirit." (Romans 8:1-2) There are times when we need to make "Seeking Him" our highest priority. Sometimes we offer up a short prayer. While this is not a formula for spiritual health, it may "get you by" in the midst of a busy schedule. But we need extended time with the Lord, when we can open our hearts to Him, and have Him open His heart to us.

Guilt creates a feeling of condemnation, but freedom from condemnation produces confidence in our prayers. Once we confess our sins, He is "Faithful and just to forgive us our sins, and to cleanse us from all unrighteousness." (1 John 1:9)

"If I had cherished sin in my heart, the Lord would not have listened." (Psalms 66:18)

If you have lived with unforgiveness in your life and have allowed this to rule your spirit, this will be a hindrance to your spiritual blessing and a stronghold that stops the power of God from flowing to you. By asking forgiveness, you are easing the offense. God will blot it from any record in heaven and will cleanse it out of your spirit. The enemy Satan may attempt to bring back a memory of sin for a season, but the Holy Spirit will rise up and remind you that you need not remember the sin that God has forgotten. If your heart senses a feeling of guilt, then immediately repent and ask God for forgiveness and cleansing. This action will keep you humble before God, as well as pure in mind and spirit.

I believe the most perfect way of receiving anything from the Lord is through your own personal faith in the Word. God is true to His Word. He has magnified His Word above His name. (Psalms 138:2) The word "confess" literally means "to agree with." Confession means coming into agreement with God about our sin. It means admitting that we have sinned and that it was wrong. It means viewing sin as God does. God promises that if we will come into agreement with Him over our sin, He will act, on the basis of Jesus' blood, to cleanse us and fully restore our fellowship with Him. Confession brings cleansing, healing, and restoration.

To come freely into God's presence, you need to know that Jesus' blood has paid your debt. In the courts of heaven, the penalty has been paid and your case has been closed. You need to admit you were wrong, and receive the forgiveness Jesus has already purchased. When that is done, you are free to enjoy God's presence.

Dealing with those who cause you grief begins with asking God to bring to your mind that person who has grieved you, hurt you, and whom you have not forgiven. Then, ask God to forgive you for the sin of not forgiving that person. Now forgive that person, asking God to give you the strength and ability to forgive. Now ask God for as much love as He wants you to have for the person who grieved you. Next, ask God how you should confirm your love for that person. Wait in silence for His answer. Pray, promising God that you will do whatever He has told you to do. Now go do it!

Forgiveness

Let's read a few scriptures concerning forgiveness

"If thou, Lord, shouldest mark iniquities, O Lord, who shall stand? But there is forgiveness with Thee, that thou mayest be feared."(Psalms 130: 3, 4)

"I, even I, am He that blotteth out thy trans-gressions for Mine own sake, and will not remember thy sins." (Isaiah 43:25)

"For if you forgive men their trespasses, your heavenly father will also forgive you." (Matthew 6:14)

"And you, being dead in your sins and the uncircumcision of your flesh, hath he quickened together with Him, having forgiven you all your trespasses, having canceled out the decrees against us and which were hostile to us, and He has taken it out of the way, having nailed it to the cross." (Colossians 2:13, 14)

"And he answered and spake unto those that stood before him, saying, Take away the filthy garments from him. And unto him he said, Behold, I have caused thine iniquity to pass from thee, and I will clothe thee with change of raiment." (Zechariah 3:4)

Key Points

Strife and confusion are a breeding ground that creates negative feelings toward others.

If we willfully refuse to forgive, God cannot and will not forgive us.

God does not release us to pray for other needs until we clean up our lives by confessing our sins.

Forgiveness is required before you can enjoy emotional, spiritual and physical healing.

Guilt creates a feeling of condemnation, but freedom from condemnation produces confidence in prayers.

Notes

Chapter 4

A Humble Heart

The scriptures tell us that the humble hear and understand the voice of God. To be humble means you are not boastful. Humility is one of the greatest qualities of all the great Bible characters. Humility is the pathway to intimacy with God. "Though the Lord is on high, he looks upon the lowly, but the proud He knows from afar." (Psalms 138:6)

If we are humble, God will "look" on us, meaning He will be intimate with us. If we are proud, we will not hear His voice. He will deal with us at a distance. Humility is believing in our hearts that our best qualities are not good enough for us to deserve God's attention, or even to gain us the lowest position of service to Him. Humility is seeing ourselves, not in comparison with one another, but in the light of God's great awesomeness. John the Baptist said of Jesus, "He must become greater; I must become less." (John 3:30)

Humble people want to obey God, even when obedience is painful. Our willingness to do whatever He tells us encourages Him to speak to us and enables us to recognize and understand His voice. Humble hearts are never satisfied with obedience alone. They want an intimate friendship with God; they want His friendship more than anything else. The Lord longs for friends with whom He can share His secrets. Good friendships do not just happen, they are cultivated over a period of time, and they are often painful. They take time because trust grows slowly.

God speaks to us and enables us to hear Him clearly. It is the humble, not the smart, whom God guides and teaches. When it comes to hearing God, humble people seek to obey God, be friends with God and to pray. They long for an open communication with the Lord, they want to pray, meditate and think upon the things of the Lord every chance they get. Praying is one of the most practical things we can do. Humble people seek to pray. They ask God to reveal things to them. "Call to me and I will answer you and tell you great and unsearchable things you do not know." (Jeremiah 33:3)

If you want to unlock the meaning of humility, the book of Daniel shows us how Daniel fasted and prayed, expressing his humility in his friendship with the Lord and his willingness to always obey God. He confessed his weakness and his dependence upon the Lord. Following Daniel's example is the best way to understand "Humility before the Lord." Daniel was humble enough to know it was not his work, but the work of the Lord. All credit was given to God. When the Lord spoke, change occurred, from Saul to Paul He spoke. From David to king, He spoke. From Esther to queen, He spoke. Paul, David and Esther were all humble before the Lord and they all put their dependence on God, took a leap a faith and saved nations. The same way the Lord "spoke" into their lives, He will speak into your life and the lives of your family.

Humble persistence is more important than intelligence in trying to discover what only God can reveal. Understanding what the Lord wants us to do is the reward for those "Who because of practice have their senses trained to discern good and evil." (Hebrews 5:14) As you fast and pray, search your heart to become humble before the Lord. This is a personal thing between you and God. Approach the Lord with a humble heart as you ask for forgiveness. The Lord reveals sin that is not always evident to us. When you acknowledge these unknown sins before the Lord, this creates a humble heart. You will realize that the way you have been living, thinking, and acting has not been pleasing to the Lord. Repent for everything you say, do and think. Ask God to replace the things you think about, the things you do, and what you say to become a new way of thinking, which leads to doing and saying things that are good and pleasing to God.

An example of unresolved sin is fault-finding and anger. These are not signs of a humble heart, but rather a wounded heart that has refused God's healing mercy that comes with repentance. Of course, these feelings will always resurface in our human state of being, but do not dwell on these feelings and thoughts. Asking God to remove those feelings will always sustain your humility. A humble heart will always lead to an obedient heart, thus seeking the Lord at the first signs of mental sin.

Genuine repentance always leads to obedience, which is attempting to maintain your friendship and love for the Lord intact. Celebrate people when they are successful. Success is a gift from God. In Christ, your time will come. "Therefore humble yourselves under the mighty hand of God, that He may exalt you at the proper time." (1 Peter 5:6) The law of God's love teaches us to believe in and hope for the best in everyone. Appreciating others will give us influence in their lives. If we are not jealous, we can learn from those around us who are successful in marriage, business, parenting, and just about anything else. We don't have to compare ourselves with anyone else. We can simply be ourselves and enjoy our relationships and learn from one another. A competitive environment produces envy. Philippians 2:3 says to do nothing from selfish ambition. Part of humility is to attain unity and harmony. How humbling would it be to have happy, healthy relationships that are centered around Christ? A humble heart can have those relationships.

I personally had to become humble before the Lord, understanding that I am nothing without Him. He created me the way I am. My appearance, my character, my thoughts, habits, DNA, gifts and talents. They are mine, not someone else's, but mine. He also gave me free will to either live in my own will, or His. I have tried living in my own free will, which was disastrous, and then I tried living under His will. Guess what? There is nothing like living for His will to be done in my life. I have learned the hard way, as many of you have. You may have experienced that there is no way like living under the trusting hand of God. All the storms in my life usually came without warning. I was never ready for them, but they had one thing in common: I figured out how to find Jesus in them. Whether He calls me to walk through the storm or wait for the eye of it. I have found the master of the wind, the maker of the rain, the one thing that could calm the storm or calm me down to stand in the storm and acknowledge Him. It's Jesus.

"Seeing" is about learning what to look for. With Christ, you will always find what you are looking for. If you value finding the negative, it will always be there and your agreement with it will always further empower it. You need to correct the "seeing" defect and stop looking at the negative perspectives of society and the immediate future. It is important to not pay attention to negative reports or get caught up in believing we are all going down. Seek and see what the Lord has for you. Even in the storms of life or the lives of the people around you, God will always promote people who have loved, shown mercy to others, and not cut down others to drive them into deeper darkness.

This is the time to become excited. If you have suffered loss, God will repay you. All you have to do is ask with a humble heart and He will respond. God draws the spiritual outcasts and drags a net along the bottom that will pull up people from all walks of life, including your life.

To be a part of God's agenda, we must humble and love unconditionally and be willing to walk with people who have been rejected and wounded. Every morning before I get out of bed, I acknowledge my love for my King and my dependence on Him to guide me and use me every day to bless someone in whatever way He sees fit for me to do. I ask God to search my heart and receive the love I have for Him. To have genuine love for God, you must seek to have a humble heart and understand you were created by Him, regardless of how you came into this world. Leave your past in the past and seek your future in His will. It doesn't matter what your past has been like or what horrible things you have done, humble yourself before Him. When you feel your unworthiness, then ask forgiveness, and forgive others. Now, you can seek His will to be done in your life.

Follow His lead by listening to your instinct in every circumstance. If you are seeking the Lord for all decisions with an open, humble heart, He will lead you. That small inner voice that lets you know what to do is the Holy Spirit prompting you to make good choices that please the heart of God. This is the formation of Christ in us. The fact that we will encounter trouble does not mean we are in the Lord's will or not in the Lord's will, for in this world we will have problems. "These things I have spoken unto you, that in me ye might have peace, in the world ye shall have tribulation, but be of good cheer; I have over-come the world." (John 16:33) While not every-thing is good that happens in our lives, we know that God works all things together for good. "And we know that all things work together for good to them that love God, to them who are the called according to His purpose." (Romans 8:28) That "good" is the formation of Christ in us. Trouble becomes a servant when we learn to respond rightly in the Lord's hands, in His will. In good times, in hard times, the Lord has promised to guide His people continually. It is not just in difficult situations, but also in those things we think we understand, that we need His direction.

Notice the word "all" in the following verse: "Trust in the Lord with all thine heart; and lean not unto thine own understanding. In all thy ways acknowledge Him, and He shall direct thy paths." (Proverbs 3:5-6) Scripture makes it clear that integrity is to guide the decisions we make. "The integrity of the upright shall guide them." (Proverbs 11:3) This unity within Christ in us opens up the mind He gave you to utilize it at a larger and deeper level. In a way, it's like He is using building blocks. Your mind becomes built up and attuned to what the Spirit is saying, what the Spirit is doing and what the Spirit knows.

One day, these new creative elements inside you will shift into high gear.

The first step in the humble heart is the new step, the new thing in God with a new creative outlet. You will never know the awesome stuff God has for you until your heart becomes attuned to Him, allowing the creativity to flow. The more you are willing to learn from the Holy Spirit guiding you by trial and error, the more you will become competent and effective in the Lord's will. He will honor you and your imperfections with His grace, bestowing blessings in your life.

Walking away a winner often requires us to lay aside and unload some things we have carried in our past, right, wrong, or indifferent. Holding onto these often good or wrong things of our past will actually limit our ability to step into the new creative things that God has prepared for us. We must recognize and fully appreciate that God has prepared new paths to walk in that cannot be connected to the past, as they will become burdensome, leading to pride, worry, and anxiety. Anxiety comes when we obsess about what may or may not happen. When you are feeling anxious or disappointed about something in your past, encourage yourself and reframe your thoughts to focus on the goodness of God. Meditate on Psalms 23:6: "Surely goodness and mercy shall follow me all the days of my life." See God's goodness and mercy aggressively following you and overtaking you every day, every moment and everywhere until you cannot escape the blessing. Peace will come when we obsess about what God is doing for our good. "For I know the plans I have for you declares the Lord, plans to prosper you and not to harm you, plans to give you a hope and a future." (Jeremiah 29:11) Even if you have not succeeded in previous days or years, do not lose heart! God is saying, "Try it again!" It is time to regroup and try again, knowing that failure is never God's plan. Take comfort in this.

It is very important for each of us to recognize that our relationship to the Lord is based on His righteousness, and not our own. Once we understand this, we can draw near to the Lord and commune with Him no matter how we may feel. As a result of this ongoing, daily fellowship with Jesus, we become available to Him. The Lord's part is to reveal His presence as being available to us. Our part is to become humble, sensitive and responsive to His seeking presence to become available to Him as "A willing, humble vessel" through whom His glory might be revealed.

In the same spirit of humility, giving of ourselves, God is freeing up gifts and callings that have been given to people who have gone to heaven. Many of these spiritual gifts and callings will be given to those who have been humble, seeking God, and have not built themselves up nor have operated in pride. God is lifting up those who have been humble; some of them are the least expected. Those who receive these gifts and callings will have a sudden acceleration in their life, ministry or businesses. There will be a time of refreshment for those who are weary. Many will experience mini renewals of His presence and gifts in their lives. Many people have been suffering from hope deferred for so long that they need to soften up and be recharged. A rain of the Holy Spirit will come upon those who are seeking all that God has for them with humble hearts.

This movement will look very strange, as all types of people will begin to be drawn to God. In this midst of this, a new generation will begin to awaken to God's love, power, and acceptance. This will be the start of your new season, an open opportunity for you to step up to a new level and see the results for your efforts. But people who have been building their lives, ministries, and using others for their own gain will experience decline. God's love is still with them, but they will no longer have the edge they once had. Gifts and callings will be rearranged by the Lord. The Word of God stands up for itself and it cannot deny itself. The Word of God supports and confirms itself. When Satan tries to get you to doubt the fullness of God's intentions, His promises, to doubt what God says, there is a truth that is inscribed in the Word of God forever, in His own holy language.

Humble people see beautiful things in places where other people see nothing. As you humble yourself before the Lord, you will begin to see His beauty in places you have looked at in the past. All of a sudden, the familiar becomes a vision of beauty; it's the handwriting of God.

Let's pray:

Father, open my heart to be fully Yours. Help me to follow where You are leading me. Help me to discern the times, know Your intentions, allow me to hear Your voice and follow Your lead as I present myself before You with a humble, forgiving heart. In Jesus' name, Amen!

Key Points

The humble hear and understand the voice of God.

God looks on the humble.

Humble people want to obey God, even when obedience is painful.

Humble people long for an intimate friendship with God.

The Lord longs for friends with whom He can share His secrets.

It is the humble, not the smart, whom God guides and teaches.

List what is keeping you from becoming a humble, willing vessel.

Notes

Chapter 5

For as He Thinks in His Heart, so is He

"For as he thinks in his heart, so is he."

(Proverbs 23:7)

I t all starts with what we think and say. You must realize that the Word of God has the power to change our traditions, belief systems, lies and deceptions that have been imbedded in our minds. God already has your success and life all planned out for you. "For I know the thoughts that I think toward you, says the Lord, thoughts of peace and not of evil, to give you a hope and a future." (Jeremiah 29:11)

You see, the Lord has a wonderful, peaceful plan for you. By following God's plan, you can take control and steer yourself in the right path. The true power of the spoken Word of God is beyond our understanding. A hidden secret revealed to equip God's people for empowerment, to speak into us, to speak forth to others. Our world revolves around what we think, say and do. This is a divine gift given to us to use to survive day by day. You make choices every day in everything you think, say and do that affect your life and the lives of others. You can either bless your life and the lives of others or destroy them. "Guard your heart above all else, for it determines the course of your life." (Proverbs 4:23)

"For whatever is in your heart determines what you say. A good person produces good things from the treasury of a good heart, and an evil person produces evil things from the treasury of an evil heart." (Matthew 12:34-35) Your thoughts provide the fuel for your words, and your words provide fuel for your world. It's important to know that if you do not like who you are, you are only one thought away from turning toward the Godly life you desire. If your thoughts turn towards God, you will sift your thoughts, filtering out anything that you do not need to dwell on.

You will become the master of your thoughts and desires that shift heavenward to receive what the Lord has for you. "I will put my instructions deep within them, and I will write them on their hearts." (Jeremiah 31:33) Can the Lord put His instructions deep within your heart? "Fix your thoughts on what is true, and honorable, and right, and pure, and lovely and admirable." (Philippians 4:8) You must become attuned to what thoughts enter your mind daily. What you hear affects what you think and believe. If you want positive, affirming thoughts of success, prosperity, and health, fill your thoughts with words that produce these things in your life. "So faith comes from hearing and hearing the word of Christ." (Romans 10:17)

Fill your heart and mind with life-giving, biblical truths, allowing the Holy Spirit to keep you grounded in this. Ask the Lord to illuminate this insight with wisdom in your life. It is God's will for you to live in peace and without lack, to have everything you need to fulfill your purpose on this earth and maximize your God-given potential. Seek to know, and understand how and why God has created you. Ask the Lord to reveal why you were created and your purpose. Seek to understand this with wisdom. "Get wisdom! Get understanding! Do not forget, nor turn away from the words of my mouth. Wisdom is the principal thing; therefore get wisdom. And in all your getting, get understanding." (Proverbs 4:5, 7)

It is time for you to set out and fill your mind with awesome thoughts so that they generate excitement and expectation with every word that comes out of your mouth. Because what you think is really what you are.

Who are You?

You must become skilled in your thoughts; it's the secret to life. Your thoughts and speech should be as a skilled swordsman and his sword. Take control of your life, this begins in your mind.

We must all understand that we were created to be children of God, and that we must understand the authority we have in Christ. Every battle is won or lost in the area of our minds, so we must understand to "Set the mind on the flesh is death, but to set the mind on the Spirit is life and peace." (Romans 8:6) We must take our minds off of material, worldly things and place our minds on heavenly things, relaying on the Word of God to help us do this. "This book of the Law shall not depart from your mouth, but you shall meditate in it day and night, that you may observe to do according to all that is written in it. For then you will make your way prosperous, and then you will have good success. Have I not commanded you? Be strong and of good courage, do not be afraid, nor be dismayed, for the Lord your God is with you wherever you go." (Joshua 1: 8-9) God instructed Joshua to meditate on His Word day and night so that it would fill his heart, mind, and mouth. Then He said, be strong and courageous. You see, until Joshua filled himself with the Word of God, he would not be strong and courageous.

Don't be left out in the dark from the good life God has for you. Receive the truth regarding who you are in Christ. As you follow God's specific instructions and fill your thoughts with those things the Bible speaks of, you will begin to discover the unlimited possibilities that God has for you. Inspiration is a God thing. Inspiration is God Himself speaking into our spirits. Having inspirational thoughts is God's way of finding His expression for His will in our lives.

Our lives are built by a series of thoughts and plans. Our every thought is a building block in determining our future. If our thoughts are inferior, life will be inferior, but if our thoughts are honorable and honest, we are laying the foundation for a successful and prosperous life that blesses others. What we think determines what we are, where we go, and who we meet. If you are going to walk away a winner and walk back into your God given life, if you are going to change your life, you must think for a change. You are only one thought away from changing your life and walking away a winner.

Your life is a reflection of your most dominant thoughts and what you meditate on. When you make it a practice to meditate on success, you will begin to live a successful life. You will never have more, or go any further, or even accomplish greater things than your thoughts will allow you. You must create a positive thinking environment to create this winning life. To begin this process, it must begin with fasting, praying and giving of yourself, then you will begin to think big!

You need to see yourself doing more, gaining more and being more. Vision is the ability to think with a mental image of all your future possibilities. You speak in words and think in pictures. Picture your possibilities. Jesus said that when other people were unable to see what was going on in heaven, He could. We were made in His image. As His son or daughter, you can tap into the creative mind of God and see what other people cannot see and hear what other people cannot hear. (John 5:19-20)

Purposefully seek God's wisdom so that He can download specific goals, ideas and resources into your mind. Condition your mind to accept these thoughts, and you will draw these opportunities and experiences to yourself and your family. It is God's desire to give you divine universal secrets and ideas to great success and prosperity. He holds the secret to walking away a winner into abundant living. Take the time (no matter what your age may be) to consider carefully the course of your life: Where are you going, what will it take to get you there? Write it down, study about it. Transform the thoughts and plans from the Lord into good intentions.

Turn your life into blessings by filling your life with words of faith, victory and life. When you read God's Word, take it personally. All of His promises are for us, and this means you. Come into agreement with what God places in your heart about you, your situation or circumstance by getting God's Word on it. You will be rewarded for every faith-filled word that comes out of your mouth. If there is a delay in what God wants for you as you wait for His season and timetable, regardless of why, keep your thoughts, your words and your faith in line with His Word and what you are expecting, and then just trust God to take care of the rest.

Remember, no force is more powerful than the spoken Word of God. Your faith attracts the attention of the heaven's angels to work on your behalf, while your fear draws the demons to work against you. Let your faith and the Word of God draw heaven into your situation or circumstance. If you are to make the most of every opportunity you are given, to not miss it, to be aware of God's promptings and become a willing vessel of honor prepared to receive, you must learn to control and then maximize your thoughts and words. By reading this book, you have been given the opportunity to create the masterpiece of your life, to walk away a winner for Christ. To walk back into the life that God ordained for you and your family. "God's Word is life and health to those who find it." (Proverbs 4:20-22)

We are all given twenty-four hours each day. We are to plan each day with purpose and "redeem the time." (Ephesians 5:16) We don't need to squander the time that we have. Wisdom redeems the time and makes the most of every opportunity. (Psalms 90:12) Effective time management requires getting God's heart on what is important, what is worth investing time in versus what we should not be wasting time on. God has a purpose for all of us; don't just let things happen, make things happen. Don't miss out on the rewards of well managed time, and a well planned day. God is a God of order, get God's timing and discern God's order.

Do not underestimate the importance and rewards of doing all things mindfully and in order. It is how we become people of virtue and achieve excellence. God will delight in you and show you His salvation. The rewards of order are many, according to His Word. You will know when to take hold of an idea and run with it. The Holy Spirit will guide you as you walk away a winner, walking into kingdom success and prosperity, once you press out of your old situation or circumstance and begin to rise to a new spiritual level with a greater capacity and clarity to influence your world for His glory. As you progress from one level of kingdom success to a greater level in the Lord, you will go through periods of returning to fasting and prayer. Remember, nothing leaves heaven until the request for it leaves earth with fasting and prayer. It has the ability to open or close spiritual doors on our behalf. Becoming successful in the Lord will only happen after you have successfully fasted, prayed, ordered your thoughts and words and managed your time, giving of yourself and your money. When all these components work together, you will become empowered in the Lord, having the ability to bless others in many ways, and that is who you are, a blessing to others!

Key Points

It all starts with what we think and say.

God already has your success and life all planned out for you.

For whatever is in your heart determines what you say.

Fill your heart and mind with life-giving, biblical truths, allowing the Holy Spirit to keep you grounded.

You must become skilled in your thoughts; it's the secret to life.

Your thoughts and speech should be as a skilled swordsman and his sword.

When you make it a practice to meditate on success, you will begin to live a successful life.

Notes

Chapter Six

First Fruit Giving

God has many good things for you. He really wants you to be blessed, but too often we lose sight of the fact that it is not our abilities that allow us to prosper and succeed, but it is God who blesses and God who empowers. "And you shall remember the Lord your God, for it is He who gives you power to get wealth that He may establish His covenant which He swore to your fathers, as it is this day." (Deuteronomy 8:18) God should always be magnified, as we prosper as a direct response to trusting Him. I am not implying that there will never be difficult times or bad things that will happen. Yes, bad things do happen to good people.

What is the true meaning of prosperity and favor? God's prosperity is really about everything in your life; it has to do with much more than just your finances. "Beloved, I wish above all things that thou would prosper and be in health, even as thy soul prospered." (3 John 1:2) My brother in Christ, Ronald Wilson from Covington, Louisiana, always told me after quoting this scripture that I needed to understand how my soul, my mind, my will, and my emotions felt, and that my outward life was a reflection of the condition of my soul. So if my soul, mind, and emotions are prospering, then the other areas of my life should also prosper in this like manner. Favor will promote you, it will give you access to places that have been closed off to you. It will do for you what your resume cannot do for you, what money, or a mate cannot do for you. Favor is undeserved access. It takes you places you may not be qualified to go otherwise, only the favor of God can get you there. As you give, God will bless you with tremendous favor! I personally know what it is to live in a place of "lack," and I also know what it is like to live in "abundance." I don't want anyone to live in "lack" I want you to live in the abundant life Jesus spoke about in John 10:10. Remember, abundance is not just limited to financial increase, just as lack is not limited to only affecting your finances. Likewise, abundance relates to every area of your life.

What are your reasons for lack? Is there any lack of joy, lack of restoration, lack of peace, or lack of anything that God has for you? Then you must try to find out what is the cause of your lack so you can get past your season of living in lack.

The Bible says, "Poverty and shame shall be to him that refuses instruction; but he that regards reproof shall be honored." (Proverbs 13:18) Are you un-teachable? Can you accept criticism? Are you accountable? Do you lack knowledge? The Bible says, "My people are destroyed for lack of knowledge." (Hosea 4:6) We should all be teachable; we must maintain a teachable spirit, ever learning, ever humble before the Lord, seeking His knowledge. Stop reading now and ask the Lord to forgive you for being un-teachable, unaccountable, and to give you a humble, teachable heart that seeks His knowledge. Now the Lord will honor you.

Here is another reason for lack. It's called "laziness." The Bible warns us about becoming lazy. Anyone who thinks God is simply going to rain down His blessings while they sit back and stay at home, taking it easy has been deceived.

Laziness will never allow you to experience the fullness of the promises of God. It takes effort to read, effort to study, effort to work, effort to do that every day thing over and over. Stop now and ask the Lord to forgive you for having a spirit of laziness, asking Him to replace it with a spirit of ambition. Now the Lord will honor you.

Did you know that God increases the person who takes care of the poor, the person who is openhanded instead of closed-handed? Find someone who is in a less fortunate situation than you. Give to them; it's not isolated to money, it may be food, time, a hug, a kind word, or just listening with an open heart. Everything you do for someone less fortunate can be a seed sown into their life. You see, withholding from someone who has a genuine need can lead to a lack in our lives. If your motive is not genuine, stop and ask God to deal with your heart. Our God expects us to deal generously with others, trusting Him to provide for our needs. Instead of looking for a doorway or window to open on your behalf, become the portal for others and watch what awesome things will happen for you.

I want to see the promises of the Word of God manifested in your life. As you continue to read this book, ask God to allow you to grasp every meaning. God does not want to bless one person and leave someone else behind; He wants everyone to manifest the promise He has for them. Beloved, you should now sense a feeling of prosperity in your soul, your body, your mind and your emotions as the Lord wishes for us. My desire for this "wellness in my soul" feeling was generated in my heart and began to be very intriguing to me; it tugged and called out to me. Somehow, I knew in the deepest part of my nature that this was the way the scripture intended. There is a right time for all things in our lives, and there is safety in being in God's perfect timing. There are four seasons in a year, but with God there is a fifth season. It's called "your season," for in time we shall reap God's blessings! (Galatians 6:9)

So if you have dealt with having an un-teachable heart, had a renewed burst of ambition and have chosen to help the poor in whatever way the Lord leads, you are now ready for the next step. Yes, God wants to bless you, and those abundant blessings are predicated by keeping Him first in your life, an awesome principle God established for the generations through the giving of the first fruits offering. Now, this is different from the tithe, which is ten percent of our gross income earned by us. We shouldn't confuse this offering with the tithe of ten percent of our income. That, technically, is not an offering, because it belongs exclusively to the Lord. When we bring our tithe to the Lord, we really don't give Him anything. Of course, we are blessed by the Lord for bringing our tithe. (Malachi 3:7-12) The tithe, after all, opens "the windows of heaven." The first fruit offering moves far beyond the blessing of the tithes into the "not be enough to receive it" realm of supernatural increase. First fruits is a principle of keeping first things first; of recognizing or remembering God as the one who gave us the ability to get wealth. A first fruit relates to dedicated, devoted, first things. Devoted and dedicated things have the exact same meaning.

God is a God of order, not of confusion. He is very serious about things being in order in our daily lives. So, you see it's very important that we all understand this God-given principle of first things first. When you do not put first things first, everything in your life is out of order. Believe me; I have lived in an out-of-order world and in a world of His order. But, when you put first things first, everything in your life falls into place just as God promises. When we are faithful, we will be blessed. As you begin to apply this principle of first things first, knowing that all firsts should be given to the Lord, the first part of the day, the first day of the week, the first month of the year, etc., what you do first thing in the morning sets the course for the rest of your day. When you worship and thank the Lord first thing in the morning, you bring life into the order God has established. God then adds the things to you when the foundation is in place to be built upon. We are the ones who have to create and establish an atmosphere that is focused on God and based on His principles of His Word. The first sets the precedent for the rest. "But seek first His kingdom and His righteousness." (Matthew 6:33)

First fruits are also a part of God's patterns. The first fruit means the first in place, order and rank, the beginning, and the chief or principal thing, so we have to keep things in their proper order. The Apostle Paul called Jesus the firstborn of many brethren, and in Corinthians he called Him the first fruits. In the Old Testament "the first-born of your sons was required." (Exodus 22:29) Jesus fulfilled God's pattern of one for many, the first fruits redeeming and blessing those who were yet to come. There are a lot of references in the Bible to first fruits or first events. You can begin your own research into this awesome principle God ordained. The Word of God is filled with references to the first fruit blessings, but one of the most obvious is found in Proverbs 3: 9-10 as follows: "Honor the Lord with your possessions, and with the first fruits of all your increase; so your barns will be filled with plenty, and your vats will overflow with new wine." Would you like that kind of life?

This is why I devote the first twenty-one days of the first month of every New Year to fasting and prayer, seeking who to give; it's the foundation for my whole year. Without setting this foundation, I feel my year would get out of order. I offer the first month of the calendar that I live by to the Lord, to establish what happens in the rest of my year. I have chosen to honor God by giving one of my paychecks (gross amount) as my first fruit offering every year at Easter time. This is a personal choice. Some people give a first fruit offering at the beginning of each year. I have chosen Easter after prayer and seeking God. I honor God as my first fruit who arose from the grave. By presenting God the first fruits, the first part of my day, my month, my year, my first of increase, I am presenting this as holy and consecrated to the Lord, It governs everything else that operates in my life. Give to God what is His, the first of all things, and the tithe. The first check from a new job, the first of a new year's salary. Just remember God as first in all things and you will understand what a first fruit offering is in your life. Ask God to reveal everything first in your life.

Life abundant or lack abundant, the choice is ours to make. This is why the first fruit is so vital for you to understand and activate in your life. This is how I walk away a winner every year!

I pray that you will understand that God is not trying to take something from you. He has made a plan for us to follow to walk in the abundant life He promised through Christ Jesus. As you begin to receive revelation knowledge in your heart, you are positioning yourself to receive the key to unlocking many doors He has waiting to be opened by you. The first fruit offering is not about positioning ourselves to "win" God's acceptance and favor. It is about positioning ourselves to "release" God's blessings, acting in faith to see them manifest in our lives. It is your faith in Him that brings God's promises to you. Expect God to cause prosperity to come into your life. "But without faith it is impossible to please him, for He that cometh to God must believe that He is, and that He is a rewarder of them that diligently seek Him." (Hebrews 11:6) Just as any farmer operates, you should expect a harvest from the seed you plant.

This is my prayer for you as you honor Him in this significant way; "May He who supplies seed to the sower, and bread for food, supply and multiply the seed you have sown and increase the fruits of your righteousness, while you are enriched in everything for all liberality, which causes thanksgiving through us to God." (2 Corinthians 9:10-11) God will answer and reward you for your obedience to Him as your heart swells with the revelation of destiny and abundance, with an overflow of thanksgiving to our Lord and King. Since I began to participate and understand the power of the first fruits principle, I have not experienced a provision problem. Many things have happened in my life by coming into His obedience. Multiplication is released into our lives and in the lives of others. An example is the feeding of more than 5,000 men, women and children from an offering given of just five loaves of bread and two fish. Jesus blessed the offering and it multiplied and feed everyone. (Matthew 14: 19-21)

"You are blessed because you believed that the Lord would do what he said." (Luke 1:45)

Throughout scripture we are reminded of the importance of believing God. The Bible tells us that there is a great reward for those who have faith and believe in the Lord's promises.

A first fruit in Hebrew is "bikkurim" and literally means "promise to come." And the one who never breaks His promise is God! When you keep first things first through faith and obedience, you turn God's promise into provision. Because He wants to see you succeed, He has put a system into place based on the principle of "First Fruits." The Bible references first fruits or first things or devoted things no less than thirty-two times. "Honor the Lord with your wealth, with the first fruits of all your increase." (Proverbs 3:9) "When you come into the land which I gave you, and reap its harvest, then you shall bring a sheaf of the first fruits of your harvest to the priest." (Leviticus 23: 9-10) God claims the first of all things. It rightfully belongs to Him. When we apply the principle of first fruits, we see that all first should be given to the Lord, the first of the day, week, month, and the first of our harvest, be it the wages for the first day, week, or month. You can put God first in every area of your life by fasting, praying and giving. Give God the first thoughts in the morning in prayer.

Do you have a plan where you want to be in one year? Make an offering of your first fruits, plant a seed for the next year. There is a greater portion that awaits you in honor of your first fruit offering. According to Deuteronomy 8:18, "Through your first fruit offering, He gives you the power to acquire wealth to establish His covenant with us." Each year at Easter time, I put God first and honor Him with the first fruit of my substance by sowing a first fruit offering of one paycheck. That is a big sacrifice, but it is a seed for my harvest and God always provides. When you need, God knows. When you ask, God listens. When you give, God receives. When you believe, God works. Faith is the currency of heaven. It's the substance you need for God to go to work. Hebrews 11:1 says "Now faith is the substance of things hoped for, the evidence of things not seen."

First fruits has impacted my life personally and the lives of those around me. It impacts my family as a generational blessing I am passing down to the children and my children's children. (Proverbs 13:22) A first fruit is more than just an offering, it's a life principle. I challenge you to put first things first and honor God. Start activating the Word of God by offering to Him; you will set a precedent of what will come. You will release a great promise of provision as a direct result of your obedience. Just give your very best offering that God places on your heart. The results are miraculous!

The Word of God has been spoken, the evidence is mounting! Come with your first fruit offering, prove God, the promise is yours. Watch Him pour out more blessings than you can hold, which means you will have to share with others. You can build a powerful "more than enough" heritage, starting with your loved ones and pass it down to your future generations. The Bible says, "A good man leaveth an inheritance to his children's children; and the wealth of the sinner is laid up for the just." (Proverbs 13:22) God can use you and your family to build a mighty heritage as you grow into deeper knowledge and wisdom. "May the Lord, the God of your fathers, increase you a thousand-fold more than you are and bless you, just as He has promised you." (Deuteronomy 1:11) Obviously, the Lord wants to bless us and our families with long life and peace, just as He does with His many other blessings. Our part is to walk in faith and obedience. "The blessing of the Lord, it maketh rich, and he addeth no sorrow with it." (Proverbs 10:22) Amazing things are just ahead, generosity buys happiness! Are you ready to walk away a winner?

Key Points

Remember, abundance is not just limited to financial increase, just as lack is not limited to only affecting your finances. Likewise abundances relates to every area of your life.

Four seasons in a year, but with God there is a fifth season. It's called "your season."

A first fruit is a principle of keeping first things first. A first fruit relates to dedicated and devoted first things.

God is a God of order, not confusion.

A first fruit in Hebrew is "bikkurim" and means "promise to come."

Generosity buys happiness.

Examine your checkbook.

Notes

Chapter 7

Hearing the Voice of God

At this point of your fast, you should be in a prayerful state. You have already gone through conviction of your sins and asked God to reveal sin; you have confessed before the Lord and forgiven others. If this has not happened, stop! Go back over the chapter on forgiveness and repent. Ask the Lord to supernaturally reveal sin. Perhaps you feel convicted, but don't really understand what sin is holding you back. The Lord can show you underlying sin that is not apparent to you. Now seek Him and repent.

The Holy Spirit is the only person powerful enough to break through the darkness of the human heart with a conviction of sin, which leads to repentance. (John 16:8) God is looking for humble, clean hearts to use as His vessels. Now you can begin to start praying to hear the voice of the Lord. Ask God to speak to you through dreams, visions, scriptures and other avenues of communication. Don't be afraid to ask the Lord for His will in your life. Relax; it's not scary or creepy. The Lord can minister to you in many ways. Pray for the Lord to open the eyes of your heart, clear your mind, and prepare your soul to receive all the goodness He has for you. God is a very special person living in our special time.

If you don't know where to start, a good place would be the Bible. So many of us have been conditioned to not read the Bible or to read it in terms of our experience rather than in terms of the experience of the people in the Bible. If we don't hear God's voice today in special ways, we assume He is not speaking in special ways. If we don't see miracles today, we assume He is not doing miracles anymore. Yet, the Bible is filled with dreams, visions, miracles and many other supernatural experiences. Some church-goers simply deny that things even happened. They say these stories are myths that were never meant to be taken literally; they were just meant to illustrate great theological truths. Two sad effects result from reading the Bible in such an anti-supernatural manner.

First of all, we will experience very little of God's supernatural power. It's because we have neither the faith to pray for miracles nor the con-fidence that God can speak to us in any super-natural way He chooses. It can be because our method of reading the Bible has taught us not to expect these things. Beyond taking us to heaven, we don't expect too much from God. And usually we get what we expect. It can be hard to read a book that tells us how God supernaturally intervened in the daily lives of His children, and yet see no practical relevance for these supernatural phenomena in our present experience. Once the supernatural element is taken out of Bible, it becomes merely a moralistic life guide. And God becomes a remote God who helps His people, but not very much.

The Bible was given to us that we might hear God's voice and respond to the voice with life-changing faith. Yet, it is all too common for Bible-believing people to read the Bible without ever hearing that voice spoken to us in many ways. There are a number of examples from the New Testament that show us God still speaks today in ways other than the Bible, examples from the lives of Jesus, the apostles, and others. It would be easy to discount these examples by saying, "These were special people living in special times." But this would be a very unbiblical way of reading the Bible. A more biblical way is to think of Jesus as our supreme example of both how to live and how to minister. Most of my life I've made the mistake of believing God for too little until I began fasting, praying and giving. "Everything is possible for him who believes." (Mark 9:23)

Secondly, some Christians live all their lives without ever consciously experiencing a direct communication from the Father, Son and Holy Spirit, or even the angels. They are so used to reading the Bible in terms of their own experience that it is easy for them to miss the book of Acts' superstar character, Luke. When they read the Bible, their lack of supernatural communication with the Lord filters out Luke's emphasis on divine supernatural communications between God and His servants. Throughout the book of Acts, there is supernatural communication from God to His servants. In the New Testament, the word "revelation" refers to a secret God has made known. When God reveals something, He is showing us something we could never ever know, or did not know, through natural means. The ultimate source of revelation in the early church is God the Father. He is the one who poured out the Holy Spirit (Acts 2:17) and who anointed Jesus of Nazareth with the Holy Spirit and power. (Acts 10:38) However, when God chooses to reveal something to one of His servants in the book of Acts, the agents of revelation are the Holy Spirit, Jesus or the angels.

The Holy Spirit may speak directly to certain people, telling them where to go and what to do (Acts 8:29; 10:19-20), or He may speak to a whole congregation. The Holy Spirit can hinder or stop a missionary team or group when they want to leave a geographical area that is still in the will of God. (Acts 16:6-7) The Holy Spirit may compel someone to go to a certain area. (Acts 20:22) The Holy Spirit may warn ahead about suffering that will go with the fulfillment of a servant's task. (Acts 20:23)

The Holy Spirit may also inspire a sermon, give an account of healing (Acts 4:8), the filling of the Holy Spirit, and the power of God speaking through an individual. (Acts 11:28, 21:4) Jesus appears to Stephen as he is being stoned to death, (Acts 7:55) and to Paul on the road to Damascus. (Acts 9:3-6; 22:6-12; 26:9-16). The Lord also appeared to Ananias and gave him special instructions for his ministry to Paul. (Acts 9:10) Jesus appeared to Paul and gave him directions, comfort and encouragement. (Acts 18:9-11; 22:17-21; 23:11) Angels became very famous for engineering jail breaks (Acts 5:19-20; 12:7-11), and appearing to several servants of the Lord with specific directions. (Acts 8:26; 10:4-6; 27:24)

Luke was teaching his readers that neither they nor the early church could do without God speaking to them in all the diverse ways characteristic of our omnipotent and omniscient God. Some may think that this is not normal Christianity; they believe that those events only happen once in a while, so very infrequent that they should not even be considered important ways of listening to God. Once you read the book of Acts with an open mind that comes with clarity while fasting, you would understand that the stories illustrate how Christians lived immediately after Jesus had gone to the cross and been resurrected. The book of Acts doesn't deal in theories about how Christian life should be lived. It gives us a realistic portrayal of how the first century Christians really lived. You can determine how common the supernatural revelation was to them, and it is here now for us.

Luke stressed the creative ways in which the Lord spoke to him in every circumstance, he warned, delivered, guided, inspired, comforted, prepared, and predicted. If we are not experiencing these things, it is our experience of God that is abnormal. If all things are possible for them who believe, and the book of Acts shows us these possibilities, then shouldn't we make the Christianity of Acts our goal? The very same thing could happen to you if you gave God a chance to speak to you as He did to those in Acts. Apparently, the Lord enjoys speaking in a variety of ways and expects us to listen to any way in which He chooses to communicate. The more of His ways that we can hear, the more we will hear. Remember, it is always God who takes the initiative and opens a person's heart to believe.

The most common way the Holy Spirit reveals Jesus and speaks to us today is through the Bible. No one has ever said it better than the Apostle Paul. "All scripture is God breathed and is useful for teaching, rebuking, correcting and training in righteousness, so that the man of God may be thoroughly equipped for every good work." (2 Timothy 3:16-17) Jesus is telling us that the primary way He will be known is through the scriptures. This is the primary benefit of the Bible, it reveals Jesus to us. The only people who will ever have the divine success the Lord wishes to give them in this life are those who treasure His Holy Word. And the greater the responsibility God gives to individuals in His kingdom, the greater their need to meditate on His Word.

The person who does that "is like a tree planted by streams of water, which yields its fruit in season and whose leaf does not wither. Whatever he does prospers." (Psalm 1:3) People who are successful at resisting the lust, greed and temptations of the world are the ones who treasure the Word of God in their hearts. (Psalm 119:9-11) The only ones who will successfully persevere through trials are those who love the Word of God. The psalmist said, "If your law had not been my delight, I would have perished in my affliction." (Psalms 119:9) "Great peace have they who love your law, and nothing can make them stumble." (Psalms 119:165) All of these benefits and more are given by the Holy Spirit to the person who consistently visits the Word of God with a pure spirit.

There is no book like the Bible, and no substitute for regular meditation in the scriptures. The Holy Spirit is committed to nourishing and washing our hearts by the words of the Bible. Reading and attempting to obey the Bible without having confidence in God's words robs the Bible of its power. Reading the Bible with a lack of confidence can cancel out many of the benefits. Not only do we need to have faith and confidence in the Bible, we need to read it for the right reasons. C.S. Lewis wrote that when we come to the scripture it's not a "question of learning a subject but of steeping ourselves in a personality." In other words, our primary purpose for meditation on the Bible should be to meet Christ, to hear His voice, and to see Him more clearly that we might love Him more passionately. (Proverbs 3:5-6) "Trust in the Lord with all thine heart; and lean not unto thine own understanding. In all thy ways acknowledge Him, and He shall direct thy path." Ask the Holy Spirit to open your eyes to see and hear wonderful things in the Bible. Scripture reading is meant to aid in the process of "forming Christ within us." (Galatians 4:19)

Anyone who wants to hear God's voice on a regular basis will have to become acquainted with the written word of God. At times the Lord has used the words of the scriptures to keep me on track, to prevent me from causing grief or harm to others, taming my tongue and reminding me to love others.

Sometimes the Lord may speak to us through circumstances that have nothing to do with us. When we find our attention being drawn to a specific event or circumstance, we should become very alert to the possibility that God may be speaking to us through it to help others, give a word of wisdom or encouragement. A wise person possesses the skill of being able to hear from God and speak through those events of everyday life to help others. Read Psalm 37. It is one of the wisdom chapters. As a result, the Holy Spirit will speak to you, guide you and lead you in everyday circumstances. Yes, even the most ordinary Christian can acquire this instant communication with the Lord as He provides encounters that serve as windows for our souls to catch a glimpse of heaven and hear His voice. The Lord may already be doing this with you, but you have trained yourself to ignore Him and get on with your daily business of life. You need to be always looking and listening, for His voice will break through when you least expect it. Do not hesitate to act on it, the Lord will never steer you wrong. Knowledge of the Bible acts as a filter through which the events of our daily lives must pass before we can discern if God is speaking in those events. The Holy Spirit will prompt you to intervene when it's from God.

Jesus called the Holy Spirit the "counselor the Spirit of Truth" (John 14:16 – 17) because:

He "will teach you all things" (John 14:26).

He "will remind you of everything I have said to you" (John 14:26)

He "will testify to you about me" (John 15:26)

He "will guide you into all truth" (John 16:13)

He "will tell you what is yet to come" (John 16:13)

The Holy Spirit teaches, reminds, testifies, guides and speaks the truth about the past, present and future!

The key that unlocks this power of the scriptures in a person is to put your confidence in God's Word to teach you the Bible, not your ability to interpret it. "Open the eyes that I may see wonderful things in your law," prayed the psalmist (Psalms 119:18). Many times throughout this psalm, the writer asked the Lord to teach him the word, to give him understanding of the word, or to help him follow the word. He knew he would never understand or follow the word apart from the teaching and empowering ministry of the Holy Spirit.

The New Testament authors felt the same way. Paul told Timothy, "Reflect on what I am saying, for the Lord will give you insight into all of this." (2 Timothy 2:7) The first step for understanding and applying scripture is to reflect, consider, and meditate on the scripture. Then come before the Lord in humility, acknowledging our

foolishness and ask Him for wisdom to understand and apply the scriptures to our lives.
"Those who ask for wisdom in this way will never
be turned down." (Proverbs 2:1-10, James 1:5-8)

The apostles had to learn by experience how
much they needed the Holy Spirit to help them
understand scriptures; this applies to us in our
daily lives. We don't have to be nervous about
God speaking to us through the daily events of
our lives if the Spirit of Truth operates within us.
Give yourself to the discipline of awareness and
you will begin to hear the voice of God in the
most mundane experiences, such as the voice
that led me to write this book.

At the very last day of my twenty-one-day
fast, at 8:00 AM, the Lord presented this book to
me, not in its entirety but in summary, a revelation of spiritual thoughts, feelings and emotions
of my own heart, I had to share. A message that

moved me to bring my life in harmony with the Word of God and what was hid in my heart.

The clearer the revelation, the harder the task. I immediately experienced the feeling of excitement. Could I really put into words what was in my heart? I had a tablet with me in the car that moment and I began jotting down notes, words and a possible title to my book. Thoughts were flooding my mind, but I knew from past experiences that when God speaks to you most clearly, it usually means you are going to go through such a difficult experience that later you will need to be absolutely certain God had spoken to you, If fact, the clarity of the prompting may be the one thing that gives you the power to endure the testing that will follow. I was excited but full of dread. "Okay," I thought, "I need confirmation from God." So, I began to pray for some kind of confirmation, a dream, a phone call, maybe someone else could mention something to me that would relate to this idea. The very next day I checked my emails and the first email was an advertisement from Xulon Publications. Wow, there was my confirmation! I responded to the email, spoke to two very knowledgeable ladies, and that is when it truly became a turning point in my life, the clarity of my revelation came to be.

The answer to this is the key to understanding the language of the Holy Spirit, whether He chooses to speak to you with the clarity of an audible voice, scriptures, radio, a mysterious dream or even the Internet. The power in the key that unlocks the meaning is a humble, repentant heart that is ready to receive the language of the Holy Spirit. The more we understand the more of His saving power we will experience. We must diligently learn how to become sensitive to hear what the Lord is saying or showing us, even if it's from our circumstances, visions, impressions or other means of communication.

You see, the Lord knows the language of our hearts, He knew us before we were born. (Jeremiah 1:5) He knows how to speak to us, how to show us things and above all He loves us. God created us with feelings, a sound mind, and a physical body. The Lord can and does speak to us through all of these avenues, which can be a source of blessings to us. If we listen to our feelings, minds or bodies and follow the promptings of the Holy Spirit, we can become instruments to be used of the Lord for His glory. Unless we know how God speaks, we will never understand and make progress for His Kingdom. This key unlocks the meaning of the scripture that is found in knowing Jesus Christ. It's not just for highly educated, intelligent, powerful or influential people. This privilege is for all of us who have come before Him with fasting, praying and giving of ourselves.

Our attitude should be that we are available to God with an expectation that He will speak to us and use us for His Glory. "Speak, for your servant is listening." (1 Samuel 3:10) "If we make ourselves available to God, he will make himself available to us." (James 4:8) You and I have a destiny in the kingdom of God. Our destinies are different, but both equally awesome. God will speak to us because He knows we will obey and because He knows we need His voice to obey. As we grow in Him, we become more willing to do His will, we mature, and He will speak to us about larger areas in our lives. A character of humble people is that they are willing to associate with and serve people of lower position than themselves. He loves the lowly and associates with them. (Romans 12:10, Galatians 5:13, Philippians 2:3-4, Philippians 2:5-11, Isaiah 57:15, 66:2)

The Lord stays away from the proud. (Psalms 138:6) The Lord is intimate with the humble, but keeps the proud at a distance. Humility is the pathway to intimacy with God, arrogance and pride leads to a spiritually sad, desert life, void of the presence of the Lord. Humble yourself, make yourself available to Him and He will speak volumes to you.

Key Points

The Holy Spirit is the only person powerful enough to break through the darkness of the human heart with a conviction of sin, which leads to repentance.

God is looking for humble, clean hearts to use as vessels.

The Bible was given to us that we might hear God's voice and respond to the voice with life-changing faith.

The most common way the Holy Spirit reveals Jesus and speaks to us today is through the Bible.

People who are successful at resisting the lust, greed and temptations of the world are the ones who treasure the Word of God in their hearts.

Notes

Chapter 8

Worldly Riches

God set me free from the pursuit of worldly wealth to seek riches on His terms. To be a Christian means believing in, trusting in, and accepting Christ as Savior. Every Christian does this, but it's the next step, however, where so many of us falter at serving Christ as Lord. I wanted God to take His rightful seat on the throne of my heart. I wanted to pursue the meaning of true riches with the same passion and dedication that I once had for worldly wealth. I had grown in up a Christian environment with many biblical scriptures familiar to me, but suddenly I wanted to become a serious student of His Word and apply His teachings to my life. In my personal studies, I came to understand His true riches from a biblical perspective. God's word is clear that you can become rich, with or without money, if you are willing to make certain changes in your heart and mind. We were created by the Father to worship Him. If you don't worship the Father, you will worship something else, whether it's your job, your spouse, kids, your money, or even yourself. Don't be deceived, we are all controlled by what we love. If you love God, it's easy to follow His will in your life. If you love money, it will become an intolerable burden. We are each con-trolled by what we love. Love is the most pow-erful motivator of all and we want more of what we love. Christians should be the most thankful people in the world because we are filled with the love of the Father.

There is a false prosperity being preached and taught by some. Give money to get money is wrong, fruitless and even dangerous. What happens when someone follows this and then is not rewarded with earthly riches? They feel betrayed and turn away from God. Love, gratitude and obedience should be the motivation in our giving, not the expectation of money in return. God does not promise earthly riches, but His abundant blessing. As I began this journey into His plan, a transformation took place in my heart; I could feel the expectation of a blessing and believe it was real. It is important that you know and understand that the Bible stands alone as the most powerful book ever written about money. Since love is a matter of the heart, I was controlled by what I allowed in my heart.

"For where your treasure is, there will your heart be also." (Luke 12:34) This voluntary submission to what we love will either trap us in the world's belief system about money or liberate us to experience true riches found only in faithful obedience to God and His word.

The Bible makes it clear, if you love money, you will never have financial security. Whoever loves money never has enough money; whoever loves wealth is never satisfied with his income. If you love pleasure, you will never have financial success. If you love getting instead of giving, you will never have true significance.

Exactly what is your philosophy? Philosophy is your belief system, your worldview. It's how we process millions of bits of information that enter our brains every day, and it becomes our perception of things around us. The roots of our beliefs do run deeply, however, the power of the Word of God can change our belief system from the things of the world, to the things of God. The Lord has gone to great lengths to make His philosophy concerning money and possessions simple to us. We are to love and serve Him only, not money. I certainly am not saying that it is wrong to possess wealth. Wealth, earthly wealth, can be a very good thing if it's used the right way by someone who understands where it comes from. Too often we lose sight of the fact that it is not our abilities that allows us to prosper and be successful, but it is God who blesses us. This is why God warns us in Mark 10:25 and Matthew 19:24; it says "and again I say unto you, it is easier for a camel to go through the eye of a needle, than for a rich man to enter into the kingdom of God." I finally understood what this scripture meant; a rich person who thinks it's all about them, excluding God where their wealth is concerned, really cannot enter heaven. We do have a choice with regard to riches, however, we can become rich towards self, piling up treasures in our fortresses of false security, or we can become rich towards God, the only real source of our protection and security. The wisest, most practical thing you can do is apply spiritual truth to your life. "Hear counsel, and receive instruction, that thou mayest be wise in thy latter end. There are many devices in a man's heart; nevertheless the counsel of the Lord, that shall stand." (Proverbs 19:20-21) Only spiritual truth will transform your understanding of riches and allow you to escape the philosophies of this world. When God gives you revelation, that revelation causes you to move out in faith; you don't just sit in the boat and watch everybody else walk on water. You say to yourself, "If they can walk on water, so can I."

When we offer ourselves to Him as a response to His grace, acknowledging that we have sinful pride, no longer conformed to the belief system of this world, we will be transformed by the renewing of our minds. When our belief system changes, we change. The Bible tells us over and over that our belief system gives us strength. Our behavior, what people see on the outside, is an expression of what's going on inside our hearts and minds. We must renew our belief system with the truth of His word. The Lord gets very direct when defining the connection with our heart and our prosperity. A heart that trusts in the world's philosophies is cursed and will be like a tree in the parched wilderness. But according to Psalms 1:3, a heart that trusts in God will be like a tree planted by the water. That heart will make it through the drought. When we surrender to God's financial plan, a transformation of the heart occurs. This transformation occurred in my heart and changed my life.

God can make us rich in a way that we will give God's riches to others, not hoarding them for ourselves. These marvelous riches are to be shared on every occasion. When you work hard, knowing that by being productive and useful to others, your needs will be supplied and will bring glory to the Lord. When you follow God's principles for work, diligence and excellence in all you do, rewards are sure to follow. "Wealth gotten by vanity shall be diminished: but he that gathereth by labour shall increase." (Proverbs 13:11) Be careful to avoid feeling guilty when you experience an increase in your income or assets. Look at it as God entrusting you with greater responsibility as His steward. Use your increase to give more glory to Him. We are to be conduits to help others prosper, and then they can discover their riches in Christ. In today's words, "pay it forward."

The Bible never condemns wealth; it only warns or condemns when money is gained by doing evil or used for foolish purposes. "For the love of money is the root of all evil; which while some coveted after, they have erred from the faith, and pierced themselves through with many sorrows." (1 Timothy 6:10) The Lord wants to spare us the sorrow that can accompany worldly wealth. He does that by asking us to trust Him enough to give part of it away, so God took a risk to bless us so richly. The risk is that we might fall in love with the blessings and forget the one who blessed us. To minimize that risk, God designed an economy quite apart from the world. It's based on sharing, not hoarding or squandering. We must learn to be generous with others to avoid the dangers of trusting in our possessions. As we advance God's kingdom by practical means, we experience true riches by giving. There is nothing unspiritual about enjoyment, "Tell those who are rich in this world not to be proud and not to trust in their money, which will soon be gone. But their trust should be in the living God, who richly gives us all we need for our enjoyment. "The blessing of the Lord, it maketh rich, and he addeth no sorrow to it." (Proverbs 10:22) You see, God wants us to use our money to do good. We should be rich in good works and should give generously to those in need; always being ready to share with others whatever God has given us. By doing this, we will be storing up treasure as a good foundation for the future so that we may take hold of real life. (1 Timothy 6:17-19) God wants us to receive His gifts as a blessing and enjoy them, share them, and bring glory to His name. "Every man also to whom God hath given riches and wealth, and hath given power to eat thereof, and to take his portion, and to rejoice in his labour; this is a gift from God." (Ecclesiastes 5:19)

This may come as a shock, but God just gives some people the ability to make money, lots of money. The path to fortune and financial success is not merely the result of good breaks and the right connections, but is usually the result of applied wisdom, business savvy and quality leadership skills. They just simply attract money and customers. Now, this does not make them better than anyone else, In fact, the Bible makes it clear that "Much will be required of everyone who has been given much. And even more will be expected of the one who has been entrusted with more." (Luke 12:48) I am very grateful and thankful for men and women whose success has provided work for me and my family. "Since everything God created is good, we should not reject any of it. We may receive it gladly, with thankful hearts." (1 Timothy 4:4)

It's not wrong to be rich; the wrong is when we think we are the ones who have done it all. "If money can't buy happiness, then what does?" We all know this cliché is no cliché. We keep thinking that a comfortable level of income will do something for us that can't be done any other way. But, if happiness could be found in money and financial security, then the celebrity news wouldn't be filled up with meltdowns, rehab stays, divorces and untimely deaths. As much as God wants to bless us with wealth, He does not want us consumed with gaining it. It is not to be our focus in life, furthering His kingdom should be our focus. Proverbs 23:4 tells us not to weary ourselves trying to get wealth.

Let's talk about living in God's economy following His financial plan. "Now the one who provides seed for the sower and bread for food will provide and multiply your seed and increase the harvest of your righteousness." (2 Corinthians 9:10) It is God who provides seed for us to sow into His kingdom; it is God who provides bread for our food. Remember who owns it all, "the heavens, indeed the highest heavens, belong to the Lord your God, as does the earth and everything in it." (Deuteronomy 10:14) "Every animal of the forest is mine, the cattle on a thousand hills." (Psalms 50:10) So we now have read His Word and understand that God owns everything, and He provides for us. Just take a moment and breathe that all in, just stand amazed at the wealth of your God.

If everything belongs to God, and it does, then everything you possess has been entrusted to you by Him. And with this comes the responsibility for handling it wisely, according to His word, it's called "stewardship." I know you have heard this word before. You've been put in charge of money and materials that don't actually belong to you, but to your Lord and Master, and that should change the way you use them. First, it means finding out His plans for the money He's given you, which is what you're doing in showing an interest by reading this book. "You were faithful over a few things, I will put you in charge of many things." (Matthew 25:21) With responsibility comes reward. So let's begin to put our money to good use following the principles taught in scripture. Perhaps you're a young man or woman just starting out in life, greeting a sagging economy, or you're middle-aged, existing the best you can living paycheck to paycheck, knowing you still have got college costs and wedding expenses hanging ominously on the horizon. Perhaps you may even be headed for retirement or are retired with the assumption that you were prepared, only to realize that your retirement has shrunk to next to nothing. Anemic interest rates and the fear of losing social security have you realizing you are not prepared. Yes, this is all stressful, but even if you are in one of these places, the person who's thinking God's way can see reasons for simple joys, opportunities to stretch and grow, chances to see what it's like to live on faith and trust in the Lord. "He will not fear bad news; his heart is confident, trusting in the Lord." (Psalms 112:7) Don't let future worry ruin the present, be thankful for what you have. Giving helps us to remember who owns it all.

We need to start making better spending decisions. We're not called "consumers" for nothing.

We like buying things, we like having things, and we like eating at our favorite restaurant. But what are you really getting for the money you spend? As the month runs on and the checkbook balance runs thin, what do you have to show for it? Spend some time analyzing your spending trends. Just ask yourself: Do I like what I am getting in return? Am I bettering the lives of those around me? Or have I used my funds for things that I have already eaten up, put away or thrown away? Needs and wants are two different things, "Why do you spend money on what is not food and your wages on what does not satisfy?" (Isaiah 55:2) Try to let God steer your spending choices, think beyond the immediate need. "Bake what you want to bake, and boil what you want to boil, and set aside everything left over to be kept until morning." (Exodus 16:23)

Take a look at what is going to waste in your home. There will come a day when the money from things you could have done without could pay for something you never thought you could afford. It breaks God's heart when we spend money on things we could have done without, when we waste it, gamble it, and do things that are displeasing to our Father. This is a good time to put this book down and ask your Heavenly Father to forgive you for all the ways you have displeased Him with your funds, and ask Him to give you wisdom to make good financial choices that please Him. Ask the Holy Spirit to convict you when you are about to make a poor choice and guide you with good Godly choices.

At this point you should have repented for your wasteful spending, poor choices and neglect. You should now look forward, do not look back or torment yourself about the past. It's gone and the Lord does not remember it. This was my breaking point; this was when I realized that I had to move forward, repenting from all I had done with what belonged to the Lord. I now wanted to live in His financial system so I had to make changes in my lifestyle. I always had spent too much at Christmas time. With four children I overindulged in buying gifts to put under the Christmas tree. This was the first thing the Lord convicted me of wasteful spending. The whole mood of trips to the mall, the excitement, the squeals of delight on Christmas morning, and the picture taking was all an extravaganza that was short-lived, but with long-lasting financial stress. I needed to balance out my Christmas plans before I got carried away again.

So, I prayed, asking the Lord to guide me with my Christmas spending. I was led by the Lord to go to the bank and start a Christmas club that automatically withdrew $50 each month from my checking account and was delivered to me at the beginning of the holiday season. I now had my Christmas budget and had to discipline myself to only purchase gifts and holiday spending within the allotted amount of money. In the beginning it was hard; I always saw something I imagined that my child would want. I prayed each time I was tempted to spend more than what the Lord initially placed in my heart to spend. With the Lord's help, I learned to enjoy my Christmas holiday and gift giving within my means. I realized that I was enjoying the same excitement of shopping, gift wrapping and picture taking that I had felt before, without the debt or regrets. With joy and generosity, yes, but with a realistic restraint. I was using common sense in my purchasing, allowing the Lord to guide me. "Teach me good judgment and discernment, for I rely on your commands." (Psalms 119:66) This was just the beginning of my new life living in God's financial system and not the world's system. I began to pray about every situation that came up, birthdays, anniversaries, graduations and holidays, asking the Lord to guide me in my spending and giving.

Get your God-given plan and stick to it. You will be so surprised with how much you can save and experience the blessings of accomplishment. "Wisdom is the principal thing; therefore get wisdom; and with all thy getting get understanding." (Proverbs 4:7) Now that we have covered the annual spending events that occur in each of our lives, analyze the rest of your spending habits and ask God to show you how to deal with it.

The allure of getting rich, or even just the desire to get ahead, can lead you to make decisions that aren't really in your best interest, such as choosing the company of possessions over people, or choosing your own plans and ambitions over God's. Don't worry, we have all done this. Every flash of temptation I experienced was an opportunity for me to call out to God, to seek help from His Spirit within me. I realized that the Lord was there to help me avoid the temptations I was facing. "Do not bring us into temptation, but deliver us from the evil one." (Matthew 6:13)

"I think I can probably afford it, can't I?" Informed decisions are the best decisions. The Lord says, "Which of you, wanting to build a tower, doesn't first sit down and calculate the cost to see if he has enough to complete it?" (Luke 14:28) Knowing your limits is a good thing, so do things in the proper order and don't forget who you are really dependent on. Learn to pray about every financial decision, no matter how big or how small, and He will guide you in all financial decisions. Feel free to spend money in worthwhile ways after you have spent time with the Lord making your decision. "Trust in the Lord and do what is good; dwell in the land and live securely." (Psalms 37:3) So when we faithfully pay our bills in full and on time, we honor God. When we bring home groceries to feed our family, we honor God. When we spend money to educate our children, we honor God. When we pay our taxes, we honor God. "Render therefore unto Caesar, the things that be Caesar's, and unto God the things which be God's. " (Luke 20:25) When we respect the people who hire us, we honor God.

You can handle your money with a Godly holiness every time you touch it, even in the daily ways. In helping others, you bless the Lord;

seek people to bless in His name. "Whatever you did for one of the least of these brothers of mine, you did for me." (Matthew 25:40) Jesus said, "It is more blessed to give than to receive." (Acts 20:35) We need to learn something about the heart of God. He gravitates toward the weak and helpless, the poor and needy. He always made special provisions for the widow, orphan, slave and the foreigner, including those who did not have family, or anyone else in need. God increases the openhanded person who takes care of the poor. "Blessed is he that considereth the poor; the Lord will deliver him in time of trouble." (Psalms 41:1)

We have talked about self-control and managing our funds, asking for the Lord's intervention in our financial situation. Now, let's talk about biblical requirements that will keep us in line with God's word, leading us to obedience with our finances. Everyone's on equal standing with God. His word says, "The rich and the poor have this in common; the Lord made them both." (Proverbs 22:2) By offering money, we offer ourselves. "I will sacrifice a freewill offering to you. I will praise your name, Lord." (Psalms 54:6) I never used to think of giving as a worship experience, but now I do. You see, your response to giving in a worship atmosphere tells a lot about where your heart is. Giving, like life, is a deliberate act of worship. Spending money for the glory of God is a form of worship; God honors it and is pleased with it. Don't be afraid to be extravagant with money. "The person who sows sparingly will also reap sparingly, and the person who sows generously will also reap generously." (2 Corinthians 9:6) God wants to bless us and make us a blessing to others. He is looking for individuals who are givers, because He provides seed for the sower, the giver. You see, every-thing in life can be a seed to be sown into the life of another person; it may be food, a hug, edu-cation, love or even your time. Find someone who is less fortunate than you and give to them. Give to help others in need, "He that giveth unto the poor shall not lack." (Proverbs 28:27) How would you like to have a life with no lack?

By putting the Lord first, you put money in its place. Understand that God is the source of your prosperity. "But seek ye first the kingdom of God, and his righteousness; and all these things shall be added to you." (Matthew 6:33) Every January, I set aside a season of private fasting, praying and giving unto the Lord to establish what hap-pens in the rest of the year. I understood when the Apostle John said, "A man can receive nothing, except it be given him from heaven." (John 3:27) When we obey, we are blessed as Proverbs

10:22 declares, "The blessing of the Lord, it maketh rich, and he addeth no sorrow with it." It is about positioning ourselves to "release" God's blessings, acting in faith to see them manifest in our lives. It is your faith in Him that brings God's promises to you. I have tried to build everything in my life on the foundation of God's Word, with the knowledge of receiving the blessings that affect my life and those of my family and generations to come. Become a person of integrity. Integrity is doing the right thing when no one else is looking. Walking in integrity, when no one else can see you, is an act of worship that honors the Lord and strengthens you for greater service to Him. It's the little things that end up turning into big things.

When you put God's will first in your life, all else falls into place, and multiplication is released in our lives and in the lives of those around us.

Of course you do not have to wait until January to start fasting, praying and giving; this can be done at any time that the Lord impresses on your heart. The blessings of God will come in so many different forms because God gives us the ability to get wealth for a purpose. "And you shall remember the Lord your God, for it is He who gives you power to get wealth that He may establish His covenant which He swore to your fathers, as it is this day." (Deuteronomy 8:18) Are you ready to truly be empowered to prosper and succeed, which is really God's desire for your life? I pray that what you have been reading in this book can position you to receive God's promises for every area of your lives and walk away a winner. "May the Lord give you increase more and more, you and your children. May you be blessed by the Lord, who made heaven and earth." (Psalms 115:14-15)

The last thing I want to talk about is a direct mandate from the Lord. Work so you can pay your tithe and offerings to the Lord. Working should never be an end in itself, for total dependence upon the world's economic system will leave you lacking. Working enables you to give, but giving is what causes you to prosper, by the planting of your seed. Malachi 3:10 says, "Bring ye all the tithes into the storehouse, that there may be meat in my house, and prove me now herewith, saith the Lord of Hosts, if I will not open you the windows of heaven, and pour you out a blessing, that there shall not be room enough to receive it." The tithe is a tenth of your income, no more and no less. So you don't really "give" your tithe, since it is already His. You acknowledge His ownership of everything you possess though your tithe. Whatever you give above the tithe is your offering, which is what moves you into supernatural "more than enough" prosperity.

This foundation is basic and unchangeable. Many years ago, I began with consistently giving my local church ten percent of my gross income and offerings as led by the Lord. What is the first thing we have to give to the Lord? Not our money, but ourselves. That is how it must begin with each of us. Do not give your money to God if you have not given yourself. You cannot buy a personal relationship with God; He can get along without your money. It is for your benefit that God requires you to give, but He has an order. He wants you first, and then out of your giving of yourself, the other blessings will follow. He simply wants to bless us because He loves us. He wants to bless us abundantly enough that we would have enough to pass on to our children's children as much as they can handle.

God the Father wants to do the same. "A good man leaveth an inheritance to his children's children." (Proverbs 13:22) God has also chosen the use of money and wealth as a means to further His kingdom. He wants to bless us financially to help further His own plans. He provides seed for the sower. The sower is the person who gives money to help others fulfill the vision God has put on their heart to accomplish. He expects us to be good stewards of the resources He entrusts us with. The Lord is looking for good stewards to whom He can entrust His money. He ends up giving us more when we prove that we can faithfully handle what He has already given us. We all must give an account of how we are using what God has entrusted to us.

Prove God, and then watch Him pour out more blessings than you can hold, which means you will have to share with others. God has a wonderful plan for your future. (Malachi 3:10-12) The Bible is filled with promises of the Father's blessings for those who understand and obey laws of sowing and reaping. "Give, and it shall be given unto you; good measure, pressed down, and shaken together, and running over, shall men give into your bosom." (Luke 6:38) As you apply His principles, fast, pray and learn to give, you can live an abundant life filled with miracles. You can walk away a winner!

"Search me, O God, and know my heart; try me, and know my thoughts." (Psalm 139:23)

Now let's pray:

Father, I come before you right now with my tithes and offerings and the revelation that this is my appointed time for an outpouring of grace, favor, prosperity and miracles. Because I am giving, you will rebuke the devourer, cancel my debts, bring salvation to my family, open the windows of heaven and pour out a blessing so great there won't be room enough to hold it all. Now, in the name of Jesus, and by His blood, every curse of poverty, lack, debt and failure is broken and reversed. Blessing is mine, prosperity is mine, health is mine, and protection is mine. It's all mine, not someday, but today. In Jesus' name, AMEN

Now is my time to walk away a winner!

Key Points

The Bible makes it clear, if you love money, you will never have financial security. Whoever loves money never has enough money; whoever loves wealth is never satisfied with his income. If you love pleasure, you will never have financial success. If you love getting instead of giving, you will never have true significance.

If everything belongs to God, and it does, then everything you possess has been entrusted to you by Him. And with this comes the responsibility for handling it wisely, according to His word. It's called "stewardship." I know you have heard this word before. You've been put in charge of money and materials that don't actually belong to you, but to your Lord and Master, and that should change the way you use them.

First, it means finding out His plans, for whoever loves money never has enough money; whoever loves wealth is never satisfied with his income. If you love pleasure, you will never have financial success. If you love getting instead of giving, you will never have true significance.

Notes

Chapter 9

Debt-Free Living

In your heart, you want to do all that you have read so far, but you don't know how to make it happen because you are so deep in debt. Well, it's time to get out of debt!

We have all been there, including me. The first thing I had to realize, however, is that God wants His people to prosper. It grieved the heart of God to see me in so much debt, struggling to pay my monthly obligations. Psalm 35:27 says that He delights in the prosperity, or financial freedom of His people. Debt has destroyed marriages, driven people to suicide, murder and bankruptcy. This is not God's plan for us. Why settle for "not enough" when the word says He wants to give us "more than enough" to meet our needs?

It's vital that we get out of debt and stay out of debt so we can fulfill the mandate given to Abraham in Genesis 12:3, "I will bless them that bless thee, and curse him that curseth thee; and in thee shall all families of the earth be blessed." But you can't do that when you are living from paycheck to paycheck, struggling to make ends meet.

One thing is very true: the process of getting into debt is faster than the process of getting out of debt. Simply put, where you are now in your finances is the result of the choices you and your family have made. Most of us have already tried to get out of debt through the world's system of bill consolidation, second mortgages, credit counseling or even bankruptcy. Think about it. You borrow money only to have to borrow more to pay for the money you already owe with interest. Continuous overspending leads to debt accumulation. Running up credit cards by reck-lessly buying anything and everything you want will only lead to a harvest of insufficiency.

If the power of debt-free living is going to flow in your life, and if you are going to start becoming an individual who gets out of debt, you will start when you recognize that God is a God who can-cels debt. You have to believe it. You cannot walk around saying, "I am broke, and I am never going to get out of debt." That is the devil's lie. If you speak that way, you will always be broke, you will stay in debt. If you're going to be delivered from debt, you must start demonstrating faith. If you don't, you will find yourself perpetually living in the minus column of life, always sending money out, and never getting ahead.

How we talk about getting out of debt is very important. We will never start acting on debt-free principles until we start speaking debt-free language. What people say usually stems from the deep thoughts and beliefs found in their hearts. So if we believe that we can be debt-free, it should be evident in the way we talk. The true power of the spoken word is beyond our common understanding. It is a spiritual mystery, a hidden secret now being revealed to equip us for an unprecedented time of empowerment and influence. Nothing can prevail against God's spoken Word. We have to start talking as if we actually believe it. But if you start seeing and believing, God will guide you into financial freedom. We believe in God for everything else, so we need to start believing that He can work in this area as well. God really cares about every facet of our life and our debt. All of this can mess us up in so many ways, so it is definitely something that He is concerned about in our lives.

You must become skilled in your thoughts and speech as a swordsman is with his sword. Your every thought about your finances is a significant building block in determining the quality of your financial future. There is a correlation between the quality of your thoughts and the quality of your life. What you think and speak determines what you are, where you will go, what you acquire and what you accomplish. If your financial life is going to change, you must think and speak for a change. When you make it a practice to meditate on success, fast for success, and pray for success, you will begin to live a successful life. You have been given the opportunity to create a masterpiece of your life. While your thoughts and meditations are the colors you use to paint the background, your words of God are the brushes used to fill in each detail as you paint the most beautiful financial masterpiece God has planned for you. It is your time to consciously paint the canvas of your financial life with whatever you aspire to achieve. "If you abide in me, and my words abide in you, you will ask what you desire, and it shall be done for you." (John 15:7) This is why God instructs us to meditate on the "Word of God."

You must see yourself doing more, gaining more and giving more, because a vision is a mental image of future possibilities. Remember, God is a creative God; therefore we are creative beings, we are made in His image. As a son or daughter, you can tap into the creative mind of God and see what other people cannot see or hear and grasp the genius of God. Purposefully seek God's wisdom in your finances so that He can download specific goals, objectives, and resources into your mind. Your success and prosperity hinge on what lies within your mind. Change the thoughts about what God wants for you. Mental missed opportunities are simply a reflection of where your priorities are. Because my priorities were not perfectly aligned with what God intended, I missed many opportunities to prosper and influence others. He wants you to live an abundant life; it is His desire to give you divine secrets to great success and prosperity. He holds the secret spiritual recipe for getting out of debt and living the abundant life He promised. Generate excitement and expectation with every word that proceeds from your mouth, saying, "God wants me to live in His abundance."

God's system is based on giving and receiving. God's system is the exact opposite of the world's system. The world's system tells you to hoard every penny you've got, while God tells you to give to get out of debt. The key is obedience to God in your giving. It is important to understand that the way out of debt is not through your paycheck, because your job won't pay enough to take care of you and everything God has told you to do. Your job is just a means by which you can collect seed to sow into the lives of those around you. The way out of debt is through giving, give to live, and then live to give. Money is just a tool that God can use to further His gospel and bless others.

The mindset is a problem for many, as they think it's okay to give every now and then, but to give all the time, never. It's one thing to say, "I want to be out of debt," but it's something different to become disciplined enough to actually get out of debt. Most people would never go to a "getting out of debt" seminar because we don't trust the presenters at those kinds of seminars. We think they're running some sort of scam or they're just trying to sell us something. Like those people on TV infomercials, they just want our money. But rest assured, I'm not trying to scam you out of your money. Rather, I am trying to empower God's people to maximize their resources so that they can make better use of the money that they've earned.

The bottom line is that five years from now, depending on your debt, you can be totally debt-free. Five years from today, you can be putting money into investments that will pay you back. You can be putting more money into missions, widows, and outreaches to feed the poor and hungry. The sky is the limit on how God might lead you to use that extra money. But first you've got to stop wasting it; your mindset has to change. You need to become a new receptacle of God's message of debt freedom. You've got a new formula to pay off debt without creating new debt. You must allow this new attitude about your finances to be lived out in new actions. Wealth is for sowing and going. God wants to bless us and make us a blessing in the earth. He wants to prosper us. Prosperity is having enough resources to fulfill God's plan for our lives. It's not just about having all of our needs met.

Jesus talked more about money than any other subject in the Bible because He knows that how we use money reflects what is important to us. Deuteronomy 8:18 says, "But you shall remember the Lord your God, for it is He who is giving you the power to make wealth, that He may confirm His covenant which He swore to your fathers, as it is this day." Joshua 1:8 says that if we put Him first, He will make our way prosperous and successful. As much as God wants to bless us with wealth, He doesn't want us consumed with gaining it. It is not to be our focus in life; furthering His kingdom should be our focus. Proverbs 23:4 tells us not to weary ourselves trying to get wealthy. The Lord gives each of us unique gifts, talents and resources, and He expects us to put them to good use. He will give us more of them when we prove that we can faithfully handle what He has already given us.

We all must give an account of how we are using what God has entrusted to us. First we must give of ourselves; we cannot buy God's favor. He requires that we surrender ourselves to Him before our gifts can become acceptable, and then giving completes and establishes our righteousness before Him. Giving is a proof of the sincerity of our love, both for God and for our fellow believers, calling down God's favor and love upon us. Giving is sowing in God's harvest fields so that finally we see that level of God's provision for His people is abundance. The meaning of the word "abundance," from its Latin origin, speaks of "a wave that overflows." Jesus said, "Out of the abundance of the heart, the mouth speaks." (Matthew 12:34) When your heart overflows, it overflows through your mouth. If you want to enter into what I have been teaching, you will have to express your faith in action; nothing will change in your life if you go no further than reading this book. At some point, you must express this teaching, if you believe it.

Go ahead and pull out your checkbook and look at all your check entries. How many of them are made out for your own needs and desires? How many checks are written to God? God wants to help you get out of debt. It grieves Him to see you in this situation. It's important that you do your part and bring some order to your financial picture. Organize your bills and create a filing system that will enable you to put a demand on your debt and create a plan of action to help you get out of debt and stay out of debt. Make a list of your debts and write down the date that you begin to ask God for the specific financial miracle you need. Knowing exactly how much you owe is vital. You must understand that God want you out of debt. If you are trapped by debt, then you are unable to help others as often as God directs you to.

It's important that you see debt-free living as an obtainable, desirable, God-given right. Otherwise you'll remain in the same predicament for the rest of your life. Renew your mind by diligently studying the Word of God concerning debt cancellation. God will cancel your debt if you give Him a chance to do so. It's only when you have renewed your mind to the point where you are operating by faith, rather than fear, that He is free to move in your finances. You need to understand the purpose of wealth as defined in Genesis 12:3 before God allows wealth to come into your hands. You see, you must be spiritually wealthy before you can become materially wealthy. A proper understanding of money reduces the chances of you abusing it in the future. As funds begin to manifest, pay off your debt, and do whatever God tells you to do with it. Once God is confident that He can trust you with His money, His blessings will begin to overflow in your life.

Remember to become a tither in a Word of God-based local church or TV/Internet church and obey God in your giving. According to Malachi 3:8-10, "Will a man rob God? Yet ye have robbed me. But ye say, wherein have we robbed thee? In tithes and offerings ye are cursed with a curse; for ye have robbed me, even this whole nation. Bring ye all the tithes into the storehouse, that there may be meat in mine house, and prove me now herewith, saith the Lord of hosts, if I will not open you the windows of heaven, and pour you out a blessing, that there shall not be enough to receive it." This makes it very clear that if you are not tithing, you are stealing from God. Just think of all He has done for you and continues to do for you, ten percent of your income is not too much to ask. The tithe is a covenant connector keeping the windows of heaven open over your life and activates the blessings and promises of God. How can you expect supernatural debt cancellation if you refuse to obey God with your tithe? You must obey God in your giving.

If you are obedient in your tithe giving, the Lord has a promise for you. "And I will rebuke the devourer for your sakes, and he shall not destroy the fruits of your ground; neither shall your vine cast her fruit before the time in the field, saith the Lord of hosts." (Malachi 3:11) This means whenever and whatever He tells you to give, do it with a cheerful heart and receive this incredible promise. "But this I say, He which soweth sparingly shall reap sparingly; and he which soweth bountifully shall reap also bountifully. Every man according as he purposeth in his heart, so let him give, not grudgingly, or of necessity; for God loveth a cheerful giver." (II Corinthians 9: 6-7)

Go ahead and test God, pay your tithes, sow your offerings and reap the bounty. God loves a cheerful giver. Make sure your heart is right with God in your giving. Give what God places in your heart after seeking Him in fasting and prayer.

I suggest that you take your gross income (all the money before taxes) and subtract taxes and tithes from that number. The rest would be your net spending income. Tithes are taken before looking at spendable income because tithes are not optional for believers. That is how it is to successfully live the Christian life. You can't live it properly if you don't begin by tithing. If God is our source, then when we ask Him, He will give us all creative ideas to create wealth and income. If God is our source, then we won't be prideful and tell everyone how wise we were in creating the wealth that God brought to us. I want to be quick to give God the glory for what He is doing.

Don't allow the devil or the opinions of others keep you from being the blessing God desires you to be. Sadly, many see financial giving as a loss. It actually grieves them to give. It grieves them to tithe. I am not trying to get something from you; instead I'm trying to get something *to* you. I am trying to position you to receive whatever it is you need from God. Purpose in your heart to allow God to control your finances, not you. Deposit the Word of God in your heart daily and meditate on it several times per day as Proverbs 4: 20-21 commands us, saying, "My son, attend to my Words; incline thine ear unto my sayings." The Word of God is the basic building block for everything in life, including debt cancellation.

God already has a purpose for getting you out of debt and putting wealth into your hands. We have been called to fulfill the mandate given in Genesis 12:3 to be blessed, so we can be a blessing to others. Desperate people do desperate things to solve their debt problems. You need to get to the point where you are so fed up with debt that you are willing to try anything. Are you at this point? If so, then try God and position yourself to receive God's promised abundance. You need to be able to see the world through the eyes of a loving and merciful God who desires to meet your needs and use you to help others. Without understanding the heart of God, your money is worthless. How can you do all of the things God desires you to do if you are buried and burdened with debt? How can you bless others if you don't have anything to spare?

The Lord wants our lives to be influential for the kingdom of God. So the question is, where can I be most influential? Pray and ask God for His strategies, integrity and plans for your future. Integrity is doing the right thing when no one is watching. It's the little things that end up turning into big things. Walking in integrity when no one else can see you is an act of worship that honors the Lord and strengthens you for greater service to Him. Excellence brings influence. Proverbs 18:16 reminds us that our gifts bring us before great people, and Philippians 4:13 says that we can boldly say, "We can do all things through Christ who gives us strength." The visions that the Lord gives you may take time to unfold. Be patient, and trust God to bring them to pass. While you are waiting, however, you must do your part by walking in integrity. Accomplishing what God puts in our hearts to do also requires us to prioritize our relationships and responsibilities. A prioritized life causes us to make the right decisions in difficult times.

There are many strategies available to get you out of debt, but only one method works without fail. You must purpose in your heart to leave behind your old ways of thinking about money and debt. Pray and invite God into your program of debt-free living. It's only through His power that you will find the ability to keep out of financial bondage. God can cancel your debt, but first, you have to ask Him, then you will have to work with Him to bring it into reality. There is no activity on earth more common than prayer. Every culture does it. Every race does it. Every religion does it. So why not ask God to help you stop the impulse buying, credit card use and ask Him to take your debt and cancel it?

If you are ever going to be debt-free, there is one basic but often difficult step you will have to take and that is to discipline yourself and stop buying stuff on impulse. Keep a written budget to discipline yourself; this gets you into the habit of writing things down. Stop using credit cards. Charge cards are without a doubt among the top reasons why people cannot escape the debt trap. The interest rates alone will keep you in bondage for years to come. Do not close the accounts, as this will hurt your credit score, but put them away and stop using them. Celebrate your victories. Every time you pay off a bill, celebrate by praising God and telling everyone about what you've accomplished. Let your small victories help you win the bigger victories, and celebrate your progress. The goal is to reclaim your money and your financial independence.

God must know beyond the shadow of a doubt that you trust Him and will do exactly what He tells you to do with the money He gives you. Your financial freedom is a gift from God, but it is also a responsibility. You will be responsible for managing your money in a way that will sustain your financial freedom and also bring a blessing to others. You will have to become adept at running your life with an ongoing awareness of the pitfalls and dangers of money, and it won't be easy. One of the hardest things to do, it seems, is to keep our own lives running in proper order. If you put into action the principles set forth in this book, you can be completely out of debt in five years; of course you will always have to pay for utilities, insurance, perhaps a car note or mortgage. At some point your mortgage and car note will be paid in full. Have you seriously contemplated just how much money we're giving away to banks, mortgage companies, and interest on credit cards? Just think about how much of an offering you could give if you didn't owe anything to anybody.

If we are going to take control of our own financial destiny, we will need to make some hard choices about spending, credit cards, and impulse buying. But if we are faithful and patient in making those initial hard choices, we can lay the foundation for a future that is full of promise and reward. Obedience and faith is the key to opening the windows and doors of abundance. Spending money for the glory of God is a form of worship. Extravagant worship is annoying to some, but God honors it and is pleased with it. Don't be afraid to be extravagant with money. The Lord was extravagant, but not wasteful. That is how we need to live: generous with others and ourselves, but not wasteful. God wants to bring great wealth to His people, but He is looking for men and women of faith who have a hunger to see His will accomplished on the earth. The Lord is looking for people who will be good stewards of the resources He puts in their hands. He wants us to be completely His. How we handle money now will determine if we are prepared for God's future plans for us. He doesn't mind if we have things, but the purpose of wealth is not just to spend it all on our desires. It's to be used to further the kingdom of God. You must realize that the Word of God has the power to realign anything that is misaligned, especially in our finances. I pray this book has given you a new mindset, and a new attitude with knowledge towards walking away a winner.

Key Points

One thing is very true: the process of getting into debt is faster than the process of getting out of debt.

If the power of debt-free living is going to flow in your life, and if you are going to start becoming an individual who gets out of debt, you will recognize that God is a God who cancels debt.

God's system is based on giving and receiving. God's system is the exact opposite of the world's system.

It's important that you see debt-free living as an obtainable, desirable, God-given right.

Notes

Conclusion

My greatest desire in writing this book is to connect people with God. God's Word has never been solely for the purpose of recording the history of what He did for His people in the past. It shows us what He intends and desires to do for us now and in the future. I hope that you have caught the heart and soul of this book and that it will bring many blessings to you and your family. I pray my readers view this book as a beginning, a starting point, a place to begin a journey of exciting discovery into the heart and the Word of God. I am driven by a passionate commitment to see people succeed in every area of their lives. That passion and enthusiasm with a genuine love for people is my fuel. The Word of God says, "My tongue is the pen of a skillful writer." (Psalms 45:1) I acknowledge that God alone gets the glory for this divinely inspired work. My goal is to take you through a journey that leads to success by fasting, praying and giving, allowing you to walk away a winner!

CPSIA information can be obtained at www.ICGtesting.com
Printed in the USA
LVOW07s0649061214

417403LV00001B/49/P

9 781498 413206